# BIG GOVERNMENT LOVE
## and YOUR HEALTH

### Exploring the Synthetic Chemical-Based
### Healthcare System

## DAVID WESTROM

ISBN: 1548220485

ISBN-13: 9781548220488

Library of Congress Control Number: 2017909749

CreateSpace Independent Publishing Platform

North Charleston, South Carolina

# Disclaimer

David Westrom, the author of this book, is *not* a doctor, nutritionist, or registered dietitian. He does not claim to diagnose, treat, or cure any cause, condition, or disease. The information contained in this book is not intended to diagnose, treat, cure, or prevent any disease. The author does not provide medical advice or nutritional advice for the purpose of health or disease. This book is not intended to be a substitute for professional medical advice, diagnosis, or treatment. Always seek the advice of your physician or other qualified health provider with any questions you may have regarding a medical condition. Never disregard professional medical advice or delay in seeking it because of something you have read in this book. The opinions expressed in this book are based only on the thoughts and personal experiences of the author.

# Contents

*Dedicated in loving memory to my father, John Westrom, and my uncle Bob, Robert Jepson*

# Preface

Human-made or synthetic chemicals are prevalent in our everyday lives. These chemicals, which include pharmaceutical drugs, food substitutes or additives, processed or modified foods, pesticides, and household chemicals, just to name a few, are promoted incessantly. Aggressive promotion, especially in the case of pharmaceutical drugs, is no accident, and it has led to an excessive reliance on synthetic chemicals in the United States. How does that reliance impact the ability of our families and friends to lead a healthy lifestyle? How does it affect your ability to make decisions related to the wellness and care of your family? This book documents the author's personal journey into a healthcare system designed to treat symptoms of disease with synthetic chemicals. The system, promoted and sustained by both big government and the companies that create and manufacture synthetic chemicals, impacts not only the physical health and wellness of your family but also the financial health of the United States. The book explores the roles, drivers, and agendas of all parties involved and the ramifications of the present system on society. The book also explores ideas and options for transforming the system in a way that will better meet the health and wellness needs of families in the twenty-first century.

# CHAPTER 1

# My Dad, My Son, and My Uncle Bob

*Learning is not attained by chance. It must be sought for with ardor and attended to with diligence. —Abigail Adams*

All stories are personal…

My story starts after graduating from college in the mid-1980s. I had grown up and spent my entire life on the East Coast of the United States but was now working my first job and living on the West Coast. I was stunned to receive a call one day from my mother informing me that my dad had cancer. Initially, I was in shock and afraid for what could come next. But in the back of my mind, while I understood that cancer was a deadly disease, I was sure that there had to be a treatment and cure that the doctors would come up with for my dad. My dad was a fantastic father and one of the kindest, most caring human beings you could ever meet. I was raised in a family of four kids, and we always went to the doctor and dentist every year for a checkup. If anyone was ever sick, we always followed the advice and direction of the doctor as if it were gospel. The doctor was always right, and questioning anything a doctor recommended or prescribed was never a consideration. After being diagnosed with cancer, my dad went for test after test, but the doctors were unable to determine the source of the cancer or the specific type of cancer and what the appropriate treatment should be. It seemed the doctors were telling him to wait until the symptoms got worse, at which point the source would become obvious and they would be able to figure it out. After he saw many specialists and went through test after test, they finally determined that he had renal or kidney cancer. Kidney cancer was viewed, at the time, as one of the deadliest types of cancer with very low rates of survival.

## *Meet My Uncle Bob*

At some point during the process of attempting to determine the source and cause of my dad's cancer, I realized I needed to learn more about the disease. I decided to call a favorite uncle of mine, Uncle Bob, who lived in Las Vegas. When I was a child, my family took a few vacation trips to Chicago to visit my uncle Bob and his family. Uncle Bob was an entrepreneur and inventor, and he knew a lot about everything. He now lived in Vegas, where he had several successful businesses based on his inventions. My initial call with Uncle Bob was disheartening. He made the following points that I had difficultly believing:

1) There is no cure for cancer.
2) We are no closer to curing cancer now than we were thirty years ago.
3) If the cancer has metastasized, which means spread into other parts of the body through the lymph nodes, there is little chance for survival.
4) Traditional treatments don't work, and my dad should aggressively investigate alternative treatments.

He was essentially telling me my dad's odds were not good, the doctors really didn't have a clue, and my dad's best chance would be to try something totally different, a long shot, potentially in a foreign country, and hope to get lucky. I had trouble accepting what my uncle was telling me, but after some extensive research, I concluded that he was right on all counts. I was shocked to discover, except for cancers that affect children such as leukemia, there was really no quantifiable improvement in life longevity or survival rates over the previous thirty years. This was happening before the Internet, so researching anything was not as easy as it is now. There was also less inclination to question the judgment and advice of the "experts," and in this case and at that time, the doctors were the undisputed experts.

## The Treatment

The treatment at the time was much like it still is today—radiation and chemotherapy. The idea is simple—burn and poison the cancer cells. The reality is that radiation and chemo kill all cells. You poison yourself and hope the bad cells die, the good cells live, and you manage to come through and survive. My dad did not survive. His cancer had already metastasized, and he died within nine months of the actual renal cancer diagnosis at the age of fifty-two. My view of the medical establishment was forever changed.

## Introducing "Quackery"

I was born with a deformed left knee. It was bent the wrong way at birth, so I ended up with multiple chunks of kneecap and a knee that would not lock out properly. I wore a brace for several years while I was a kid, but it never really deterred me from doing whatever I wanted. I played basketball among other sports and even joined the Army National Guard. The army, because of the knee, kicked me out after I nearly completed advanced infantry training. Despite this, I viewed the army as a great experience and moved forward. After moving back to the East Coast in the late 1980s following my father's passing, I had arthroscopic surgery on my knee to remove loose bodies of bone and cartilage. My surgeon was very good, but he warned me after the surgery that unless things improved, I would probably need a knee replacement before I reached the age of fifty.

Soon after my surgery, I started experiencing back problems. Because my bad knee did not lock out, my one leg was essentially shorter than the other. This meant I was like a car that was constantly out of alignment. When my back would go out, I would take muscle-relaxing drugs and wait and hope for it to improve. Invariably, my back would go out again, and I would be back on the drugs. Then one day I heard about someone called a "chiropractor." I did some research and became intrigued by something that I had never heard about from the traditional medical establishment. After having my lower back once again go out, I decided to give the chiropractor a try. After an examination and an adjustment, my back immediately felt better. The chiropractor also explained how adjustments along with stretching and exercise could not only help my back but also improve my knee over the long term. A few weeks later, I was at a routine checkup with my doctor who had performed the surgery on my knee. I mentioned my visit to the chiropractor. He informed me that all chiropractors were "quacks"; the treatments did no good and could potentially cause a great deal of harm. Ironically, the chiropractor shared a similar opinion of my knee doctor. In his view, if all you have is a hammer, everything will look like a nail. In other words, a doctor will always prescribe drugs and recommend surgery. He also suggested that doctors only treat symptoms and not the fundamental cause of the problem. Today, I see a doctor when necessary but frequently see both a chiropractor and an acupuncturist. I have learned that everyone has an agenda, but it is up to each of us to research, investigate, learn, and determine what works best for us and our families.

### Back to Uncle Bob

As I progressed with my career, I kept in touch with my aunt and uncle Bob and visited them whenever I happened to be in Vegas. These visits consisted primarily of meeting them at one of the buffet restaurants in one of the casinos and discussing healthcare among other topics. You see, Uncle Bob was an expert in healthcare and wellness, and it was based on personal experience—a very nontraditional experience. At some point following the passing of my dad, Uncle Bob began to experience his own health problems. After seeking the advice of multiple doctors and undergoing numerous medical tests at a health institution in California, Uncle Bob was informed he had multiple clogged arteries around his heart, which would require bypass surgery immediately. His cholesterol levels were through the roof along with his blood pressure. He was told that he was at risk of a massive heart attack at any time, that he probably should not attempt to drive home to Vegas, and that he also needed to begin a routine that included several synthetic pharmaceutical drugs. You will hear the terms "synthetic drug" and "synthetic chemical" used throughout this book. A synthetic drug is a chemical created by humans that occurs outside of nature. Uncle Bob listened to the advice of the doctors, but he had a different idea. He drove home to Las Vegas without incident and then proceeded to change his entire lifestyle.

## A Drug-Free Solution

Uncle Bob believed he had options, and the traditional medical establishment solution was only one option. He chose a path that, at the time, was very unconventional. His solution consisted of a strict diet, an exercise regimen, and vitamins and other nutrients specifically targeted at helping his body heal his underlying condition. He woke up every morning to fresh juice and vegetables blended in an industrial blender. He daily went on a brisk walk or run that he built up to several miles over time. He took a range of nonsynthetic vitamins and fish oil. Instead of taking synthetic drugs to lower cholesterol, he took something called red yeast rice. He eliminated anything "white" from his diet. This included bread, white rice, sugar, pasta, and just about everything that might contain sugar. He also eliminated meat and primarily consumed fruits and vegetables. A funny thing happened to Uncle Bob—he got better. His cholesterol and blood pressure readings normalized, and he grew new arteries to his heart. The doctors were stunned! How could this happen without synthetic drugs and surgery? I was stunned because many of things Uncle Bob talked about, like red yeast rice, I had never heard of. Why weren't these ideas promoted by the government and the medical establishment to benefit society? During a subsequent visit to one of his specialists, Uncle Bob was diagnosed with bladder cancer. He dealt with this in a similar manner, doing the research and coming up with natural treatments that ultimately allowed him to survive and live a healthy life. Throughout his life until the time of his passing, Uncle Bob was a vibrant, highly energetic person who had a passion for life.

## Meet My Son

One of the greatest days in my life occurred in 1998 when my son was born. As a toddler, he was always high energy, as most little boys are, and that continued into his early years in school. That high energy level was accompanied by difficulty focusing and paying attention in class. Soon, my wife and I were called into his school and asked to get our son tested for attention deficit hyperactivity disorder, or ADHD. Although the cause of ADHD is unknown, many believe it is driven by a chemical imbalance in the brain—more specifically, an imbalance of two of the brain's chemical messengers or neurotransmitters[1]. We took our son to a well-known medical establishment recommended by the school and had him tested. Sure enough, the testing confirmed that he had ADHD, and he was immediately put on a medication known as a stimulant. During the testing, my wife and

I enquired about the impact of diet and specifically sugar on my son's behavior. Our questions regarding diet were quickly dismissed, as we were told by the "experts" that diet was not a factor and that the medication would address the issue. They were correct about the stimulant addressing the issue. My son became more attentive during his classes, and his performance at school began to improve. This is not, however, where the story ends.

### Upon Further Review

I had a problem with my seven-year-old son being on a synthetic drug known as a stimulant even though it seemed to work. Specifically, he was on methamphetamines, otherwise known as speed. They can be highly addictive drugs with side effects. Those side effects, in the case of my son, were many, including a loss of appetite. The biggest problem I had was that no one in the medical establishment could answer the following simple question: How long will my son be on these drugs? Having a kid on speed just didn't seem to pass the common-sense test.

Over time, I had several discussions with my chiropractor regarding my son's condition. He repeatedly asked me to bring him in so he could check him out and offer his advice. I pushed back for some time as I did not think anything good could come out of a young child having his spine unnecessarily adjusted to accommodate the agenda of a chiropractor. I finally agreed and had my eyes opened after my son was examined. His X-rays showed that he had no natural curvature in his neck, which is not normal. Understanding that the spinal column and neck are the highway from which chemical signals are transmitted to and from the brain, and that ADHD may be caused by a chemical imbalance in the brain, an abnormal neck curvature could potentially impact my son's ability to focus. In addition to a treatment program that would bring a normal curvature to his neck, my chiropractor suggested that I contact a natural health doctor. This time, I took his advice.

## Discovering "Sensitivities"

The natural health doctor ran a wide range of tests on my son taking blood, hair, and stool samples to test for a range of elements, toxic elements, food allergies and sensitivities, and gastrointestinal health. The difference between an allergy and a sensitivity is simply one of magnitude and time. Allergies typically cause more rapid and pronounced reactions such as swelling of the throat, hives, and nausea. Sensitivities produce delayed reactions and may cause symptoms such as headaches and bloating. Because of this, it is typically more difficult to associate sensitivities with specific foods and conditions. Could a food sensitivity impact the ability of a child to focus? Of course, it could. The results of my son's tests showed that he had a wide range of food sensitivities including sensitivities to gluten, wheat, rye, milk, egg whites, cashews, barley, walnuts, sugar (of course), and other food sources. The tests also showed that he had an intestinal tract imbalance with both abnormal amounts of yeast and fungal growth in the gut. So much for diet not being a factor in my son's condition.

The course of action recommended by the doctor was radical from a dietary standpoint. I received a detailed report with a recommended diet plan that would eliminate many of the foods my son loved. My wife and I were not about to impose such an extreme eating plan on a young boy. We did, however, follow many of the dietary suggestions along with the other recommendations that the natural doctor believed would positively impact his health and ability to succeed in school. Those recommendations consisted of probiotics to deal with his intestinal issues, a nonsynthetic multivitamin, additional vitamin C, and fish oil. We also took extensive steps to eliminate as much sugar as possible from his diet. This included banning soda from our house.

Within six months, we pulled our son off the ADHD stimulant medication. He has not been back on since. This year he graduates from high school and will head to college. He was accepted to every university that he applied to. He is a kind, considerate young man who enjoys life free of pharmaceutical medications and their side effects.

### A Flawed System

The personal stories that I have just highlighted have one thing in common: much of the critical data and information that was required to make informed decisions was not readily available. In each case, a very specific agenda was aggressively promoted. I had to dig and search for information with the help of friends, family members, and technology. I had to do the research, filter through the personal and professional agendas, and determine what made sense and what didn't. In many cases, I felt that I was misled and even lied to. The truth is had I understood a few basic principles along with the underlying system being promoted by the healthcare establishment and the government, it would have been much easier for me to cut through the static, see things clearly, and make better and more timely decisions for myself and my family.

# CHAPTER 2

# Here Comes the Money

*It is said that power corrupts, but actually it's more true
that power attracts the corruptible. The sane are usually
attracted by other things than power. —David Brin*

There are over 750,000 healthcare companies in the United States employing close to 17 million people[2]. In 2015, US healthcare spending reached $3.2 trillion, which equates to over $10,000 per person. The pharmaceutical industry and the drugs it manufactures account for a significant portion of the healthcare industry in the United States. Prescription drugs comprised 10 percent of overall healthcare spending or $324.6 billion in 2015[3]. Total spending for all medicines in 2015 was $425 billion. The United States held over 40 percent of the global $1-trillion-plus pharmaceutical market in 2015 with an estimated value of $413 billion. In 2015, six out of the top eleven global pharmaceutical companies were based in the United States[4]. Approximately $150 billion annually is spent on the research and development of pharmaceutical drugs globally[5]. The United States is by far the world's largest market for pharmaceuticals by a factor of three times the second largest market, China[6]. This is despite the fact that China has a population more than four times that of the United States. Healthcare and pharmaceuticals are big business. They are also a strategic part of the US economy and a major source of revenue to the US government.

### How Much Money?

The federal government collected $3.2 trillion in taxes in 2015. Ironically, this equals approximately the amount of money spent in the United States on healthcare in the same year. Almost half of that tax revenue comes from individual income taxes. Roughly one-third comes from payroll taxes, which is used to finance items such as social security, Medicare, and unemployment insurance. About 11 percent comes from corporate taxes. This equates to approximately $350 billion in corporate taxes paid to the federal government of the United States in 2015[7]. In 2015, 17.8 percent of the overall US economy was devoted to healthcare. Using a rough calculation and some basic assumptions, if government collected $3.2 trillion in taxes and 18 percent of the economy is driven by healthcare, then approximately $575 billion of government revenue would be derived from healthcare. If 10 percent of that figure is driven by the pharmaceutical industry, then approximately $58 billion would represent the revenue contribution in 2015 from the pharmaceutical industry and its employees to the government.

The average effective tax rates across all pharmaceutical companies in the United States is approximately 19.4 percent[8]. Effective tax rate for a corporation is defined as the average rate at which its pretax profits are taxed. Based on revenue of $425 billion and an average operating margin of 24 percent, corporate taxes paid by companies in the United States that make medicine for 2015 would be approximately $25 billion. This would represent over 7 percent of the total corporate taxes collected by the government, not an insignificant amount. And this does not include additional pharmaceutical company fees, subsidies, and the taxes paid by the employees of these companies, not to mention taxes from the large pharmaceutical ecosystem of supply chain partners, contractors, and so on.

## *Put It on My Tab*

The federal government of the United States really does need the money, as it is in debt to the tune of $20 trillion. The $20 trillion figure does not include unfunded future commitments, which some estimate to exceed $100 trillion. US debt now exceeds 100 percent of US gross domestic product (GDP). In other words, our debt is greater than the value of the goods and services our economy produces on an annual basis. Our debt is over six times greater than the amount of tax revenue collected annually by the federal government. Big government and the politicians who call the shots never seem overly concerned with enacting policies or creating new entitlements that add to the debt, debt that will have to someday be paid for by our children and grandchildren. Today, annual interest on the debt is approximately 6 percent of overall spending and 20 percent of discretionary spending. Each year the government runs deficits, the amount of accumulated debt grows, and the amount required to finance the interest payment increases. The more money spent on paying interest on debt, the less money available for spending on other programs. Going forward, this is unsustainable. Whether you are a business, an individual, a family, a state or local government, or the federal government, if you continuously accumulate debt, you are eventually going to reach a point where you can't pay the interest on the debt or the lenders lose confidence in your ability to ever pay back the debt, restricting your ability to borrow further.

The options for reducing deficits and someday paying down debt are to grow the economy, which increases the amount of tax revenue generated, reduce spending, or some combination of both. Government politicians obviously have no interest in reducing spending, so they are forced to align their interests with economic growth. If the economy is large and growing, the relative size of the debt appears smaller, and there is more confidence in the ability of government to manage the debt and make interest payments. Economic growth facilitates maintaining and expanding the size of big government and the power of the politicians who run it. If the economy grows and people are employed, spending and mounting debt can continue to rise. It is debt relative to overall economic production, or GDP, that is a key indicator of economic health, and politicians understand that growth and tax revenue must come from somewhere, at least in the short term if they expect to maintain power. The wealth, tax revenue, and employment opportunities generated by the pharmaceutical industry, and other industries that manufacture synthetic chemicals, support this agenda and are critical for not only the federal government but the many states where these companies reside and pay taxes. Big government and synthetic-chemical companies rely heavily on each other to ensure their continued survival and financial viability.

### The Not-So-Silent Partner

The healthcare sector, and the pharmaceutical industry in particular, invests large sums of money to ensure that big government politicians and doctors are promoting their interests and their products. The pharmaceutical industry spent over $245 million in 2016 lobbying government[9]. This was significantly higher than any other industry. It is also a large contributor to political campaigns supporting candidates from both political parties. The money it spends, particularly on lobbying, allows it to influence legislation and ensure its agenda is aligned with the power brokers in big government. However, the amount pharmaceutical companies spend on lobbying and political campaigns is a drop in the bucket compared to what they spend marketing to the doctors who end up prescribing synthetic drugs to you, the patient and consumer. More than $24 billion is spent annually marketing directly to doctors. Forms of marketing include face-to-face promotional activities from pharmaceutical sales representatives, free samples of drugs, industry events and meetings where drugs are promoted, unsolicited promotional mailings, and advertising in medical journals[10]. Some studies suggest that the largest pharmaceutical companies now invest more in marketing than they do in research and development[11]. Is the money spent by synthetic-drug companies to influence politicians and market their products to doctors worth it? Of course it is. The legalized synthetic-drug business is one of the most profitable industries in the world with operating margins that exceed 20 percent[12].

The relationship between the government and the pharmaceutical industry is a bidirectional partnership where both groups enable and benefit from the other. A good example of big government indirectly promoting pharmaceutical companies and their products is the willingness to allow direct targeting of US citizens and taxpayers. The United States is one of only a few countries that allow direct-to-consumer advertising by pharmaceutical companies. That would be the endless commercials you see on your television every day and night showing some celebrity or other happy person touting the benefits of a pharmaceutical synthetic drug. Yes, those commercials where, at the end, the advertiser is forced to quickly rattle off the litany of negative side effects of the drug.

### *Patently Exclusive*

Government also enables the interests of the pharmaceutical industry through a system of drug patents and exclusives, which protect the intellectual property of pharmaceutical companies and ensure that they do not have competition in the marketplace. A patent is an intellectual property right granted by the US Patent and Trademark office that protects an invention from being copied, used, or sold by anyone else but the inventor for a period of time, typically twenty years[13]. In the case of a pharmaceutical company, the invention or intellectual property is around either the active ingredient or the formulation of the drug[14]. The active ingredient is the structural formula of the synthetic chemical that makes up the drug, while formulation is a restructuring of the chemical or combining the chemical with new ingredients so it can provide a new benefit. In other industries, a patent may be issued around a technology that can be licensed to many companies who compete in the marketplace with similar products. The technology may be just one of many components in a larger product or solution. While this protects the intellectual property of the company that invents the technology, it tends to not impede competition at the product level, ensuring that the marketplace is vibrant and prices are affordable. Examples would include the automobile, smartphone, and television markets. Many of the component technologies in automobiles, televisions, and smartphones are patented, but no one company or product has a monopoly on the entire product category. In the case of pharmaceuticals, often, the patented chemical is the product, and the primary objective is to keep anyone else from marketing the same product for as long as possible. Patents are typically filed as soon as possible once an invention is created, and the patent protection period is based on when the patent is issued. This presents a challenge and concern for pharmaceutical companies, as the time to complete the various drug trials and gain approval from the Food and Drug Administration (FDA) to market the drug can take an average of twelve years and cost $350 million[15]. The protection period, based on when the drug is available on the market, ends up being reduced due to the lengthy approval process, which directly impacts the revenue and profits of the pharmaceutical companies.

The government helps address this issue through additional protection provided by the FDA. That protection is in the form of exclusivity, which gives pharmaceutical companies exclusive marketing rights to a particular drug for a period of time, preventing generic manufacturers from introducing cheaper alternatives. Exclusivity may or may not run in parallel to a patent. Exclusivity periods are also different for different types of pharmaceutical products. Another advantage provided to pharmaceutical companies is the ability to sue generic drug manufacturers for patent infringement when they file an application for approval of a generic drug, automatically triggering a thirty-month stay of approval. You can probably guess that the pharmaceutical industry is highly litigious. Patents and exclusives provide the foundation for the huge amounts of money that are invested in and generated by the pharmaceutical industry.

Government indirectly optimizes the profitability of pharmaceutical companies through policies that enable aggressive marketing and a system that includes patents and exclusives. But big government doesn't stop there—it also helps fund pharmaceutical product development by providing roughly a third of the funding for new drug research and discovery[16]. The pharmaceutical industry benefits from this research by leveraging it to create new products and valuable new patents.

## Creating Big Markets and Big Profits

The US government is the largest customer of the pharmaceutical industry. Being the largest customer and chief enabler, you would think the government would have leverage and would negotiate a great deal on price. But no, the government is barred by law from negotiating a preferential pricing deal with the pharmaceutical companies[17]. The Medicare Prescription Drug, Improvement, and Modernization Act of 2003 was passed by Congress and signed by President George W. Bush as an entitlement program, estimated to cost $700 billion, to subsidize the cost of prescription drugs for elderly Medicare patients[18]. Government-subsidized customers mean more customers, more revenue, and more profits for the pharmaceutical industry. You would think it would also mean preferred pricing for the government. But in this case, pricing is negotiated by private insurance companies in the form of prescription drug plans (PDPs). The debate over who could negotiate a better deal, the government or the private insurance companies, rages on. What is not debatable is the fact that the overall market for synthetic drugs grew because of this law. The government also created an incentive for future seniors to take a pass on private insurance plans so that they can receive the subsidized pricing from Medicare, which will result in higher taxes, higher debt, or both. So, big government pays the tab, the pharmaceutical industry maximizes its market reach and profits, and big government debt spirals out of control. The present system is financially unsustainable, but as we will discover throughout this book, the crippling financial aspect is only part of the challenge caused by the symbiotic alliance between big government and synthetic-chemical companies.

# CHAPTER 3

# Monopolies and Treatments

*With all things being equal, the simplest explanation*
*tends to be the right one. —William of Ockham*

Money and power help fuel the symbiotic relationship between big government and synthetic-chemical companies. That relationship and its drivers are formed around two fundamental tenets. Understanding these tenets, which provides the foundation for the synthetic-chemical-based system that exists today, aids in understanding not only how the system operates but, more importantly, how it could impact the health of you, your family, and society in general.

### Tenet #1: You Can't Make Big Money from Substances That Occur in Nature

Substances that occur in nature cannot be patented. Drinking pineapple juice may help reduce the symptoms of arthritis. Cherry juice may clear uric acid from the bloodstream and reduce the painful impact of gout. Vitamin C may help prevent colds and the flu. But because these substances occur in nature, they cannot be patented. And because they cannot be patented, they cannot be monopolized and marketed to the public at exorbitant prices.

Having an effective monopoly, as provided by the government, is incredibly lucrative. The monopoly ensures there is no competition for the drug, allowing the drug company to set and control pricing over the period of the patent and exclusivity. Elimination of competition equals inflated pricing and profits. This is illustrated by observing the drop in the price of a drug when it comes off a patent protection period and has generic competition. In one example, the average price of physician-administered drugs declined by between 38 and 48 percent following the expiration of a patent[19]. Overall sales volume of drugs increases, however, after generic competition is introduced, showing the correlation between lower prices and increased demand. Total revenue also increases, suggesting that the system optimizes revenue and profit in both the short and long term for the pharmaceutical industry and the government.

Natural alternatives can't leverage the protections and advantages afforded by government, creating an uneven playing field and enabling the pharmaceutical companies and big government to shape and control the system, maximizing the political and financial benefits for themselves. The same system and government also controls the narrative, tending to minimize or ignore the many negative aspects of the very drugs they and their pharmaceutical partners promote. The lack of information, transparency, and choice results in oversized profits for drug manufacturers and suboptimal health and wellness for the patients and consumers hooked on their products.

## Tenet #2: You Can Make Big Money Treating Symptoms

What would happen if someone suddenly cured a disease like cancer or diabetes? The answer is many pharmaceutical companies and big government would lose a lot of money. The big money is in treating symptoms of a disease, not curing it. When was the last time a major disease was cured? Depending on how you define the word "cure," the most common answer might be polio in 1955. If you look back to the early and middle part of the twentieth century, science developed cures for numerous diseases including tetanus, polio, whooping cough, and others, increasing life expectancy from forty-seven years at the beginning of the century to seventy-eight years at the end[20]. How many human diseases have been cured in the last forty years? I can't think of any, unless you want to count chicken pox and the chicken-pox vaccine.

Today's modern healthcare system is predicated on treating signs and symptoms of diseases and conditions with synthetic chemicals. This model is designed to maximize the profit and revenue for both the government and the companies that manufacture the chemicals. Once these tenets are understood and accepted, a proper frame of reference is created around just about any healthcare situation you or your family may encounter.

## Individual Genetic Uniqueness

As Uncle Bob demonstrated, the body is designed to heal itself. It may often need help in the form of a chemical substance that may occur in nature or may be synthetic. Or it may require alterations in lifestyle that might include exercise or some other form of physical therapy. Or, in many cases, it may require a combination of the above. The question will always be: what type of help is the right type of help for the body in the context of the specific objectives? This will vary from individual to individual based on a range of factors. Every person is unique with his or her own unique genetic makeup. As exhibited in the story about my son, because of unique genetics, every person also has his or her own set of sensitivities to various substances, and these sensitivities can have a dramatic impact on one's health and wellness. Chemical substances, whether they occur in nature or are created synthetically by humans, affect different people in different ways and in different magnitudes, in some cases positive and in other cases negative. One person's salvation may be another person's poison. For example, a peanut, which obviously occurs in nature, could provide nutritional benefit to one person while causing an allergic reaction to another that could have extreme consequences, including death. Other substances, refined sugar being a good example, almost always have a negative impact on the human body, with the magnitude of the impact being the only point of contention. And again, magnitude will be different for everyone. One sugary soda may have minimal impact on a certain adult, while it could cause a young child to almost completely lose the ability to focus or even control himself or herself. Today's system, supported by government, aggressively promotes synthetic solutions as the answer to almost any problem. The genetic uniqueness of the individual, and the impact of synthetic substances on each unique individual, appears to be only a minor consideration in the development of synthetic drugs for the masses and certainly not an impediment for the money-making behemoth that is the pharmaceutical industry or the even larger behemoth that regulates and controls it, the federal government. The good news is that recent discoveries and growth in the nascent genetics industry promise to change this soon.

# CHAPTER 4

# Breaking Bread

*It is better to conquer yourself than to win a thousand battles. Then the victory is yours. It cannot be taken from you, not by angels or by demons, heaven or hell. —Buddha*

Our society seems to have an affinity for synthetic chemicals. Acceptance and promotion of synthetics goes beyond those created just by pharmaceutical companies. It extends to almost every aspect of our lives, including the food that we eat and the water we drink. Even food that many believe to be natural may include synthetic ingredients or some form of "processing" that not only degrades the nutritional value of the food source but could make it harmful if consumed in high quantities or by a person with sensitivities. Foods are chemically processed for many reasons including preserving freshness, killing bacteria, and improving flavor. Chemically-processed foods, which may include various meats, dairy products, and breads, are a ubiquitous influence on the American diet.

After recently returning from a two-week trip to Asia, I was pleased to find out that I had dropped almost ten pounds. When I informed a friend of this, the immediate reaction was "I guess you didn't like the food over there." On the contrary, I love the food in Asia. The truth of the matter is that you can lose a lot of weight (at least I can) if you go a couple weeks without eating hamburgers, pasta, and pizza. Like most Americans, my family enjoys these foods, and we eat them too often. What is the common denominator of all these foods? Bread! More specifically, the refined or processed grains that are found in bread, pasta, pizza, refined breakfast cereals, crackers, and many other foods that Americans devour daily. Processed or refined grains are grain flours that have been modified from their natural composition. This is typically accomplished by removing the bran and germ from the grain.

For the sake of simplicity, I'll use the term "bread" to cover the category that all processed grains fall under. What happens when you ingest bread? The carbohydrates in the bread convert to sugar in your bloodstream[21]. In many cases, eating a piece of bread is equivalent to eating a lump of sugar. Too much sugar provides the foundation for excessive weight gain, inflammation, and numerous health issues.

## Bad Sugar

I probably don't have to tell you that sugar is bad for you. The many reasons and the extent, however, may surprise you. First off, in discussing sugar, I am referring to processed sugar. I am not including the sugar that is derived naturally from fruits and vegetables. Sugar is processed or refined by removing molasses and various "impurities" from sugar cane. There is no nutritional value in processed sugar. When you ingest sugar, it breaks down into simple sugars called glucose and fructose before entering your bloodstream. Too much fructose overloads the liver and ends up as fat[22]. Continued bombardment of the liver with sugar can lead to diseases including nonalcoholic fatty liver disease (NAFLD). Too much sugar causes inflammation, which some believe is the basis for the formation of many diseases. Excessive sugar makes your blood toxic. The body fights back by producing more insulin, which serves to burn glucose. At some point, the pancreas, which produces the insulin, can't keep up. At this point, blood-sugar levels rise, and you may end up with type 2 diabetes or some other disease. It is inflammation, however, that is being shown in new studies to be the primary cause not only of type 2 diabetes but of many types of cancer and other diseases[23]. Reducing inflammation in your body by reducing consumption of the primary toxin that drives inflammation, sugar, is a major step in protecting yourself from disease. The body and its many organs simply do not deal well with sugar. And bread is not the only food source that efficiently converts to sugar in the blood. Starches such as fried potatoes are also high on the glycemic index or GI, which is a way of measuring the blood-glucose-raising potential of a food.

## Big Government Food Groups

When I was young, consumers were continuously hit with government-sponsored promotions about the basic food groups. The four basic food groups consisted of vegetables and fruits, meat, milk, and cereals and breads. The point the government was making in promoting the food groups was each group had nutritional value, and citizens were encouraged to draw from each group to maintain a healthy lifestyle. In 1992, the US Department of Agriculture (USDA) changed things up by publishing the Food Guide Pyramid, which went further by recommending daily serving sizes for each of the food groups[24]. This created controversy, as many of the groups subsidized by the USDA (bread, meat, and dairy industries) were concerned that government recommendations on serving sizes would adversely affect their markets.

In 2005, the Food Guide Pyramid was replaced by MyPyramid where all food groups were stacked vertically, implying that they were equally important. The "Bread,

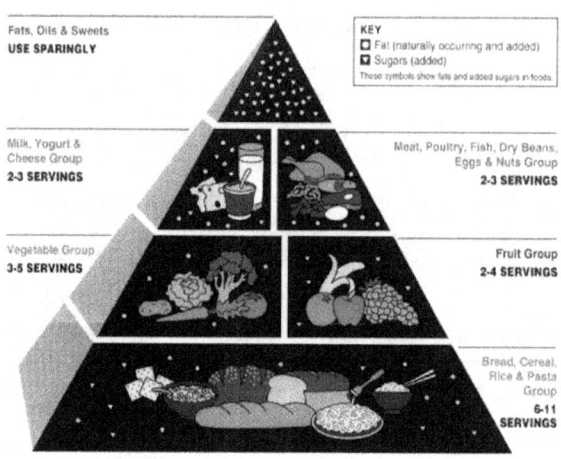

Cereal, Rice, and Pasta" group was replaced by "Grains," even though the bread items were displayed in the picture. The pyramid also included steps on one side to emphasize the importance of exercise.

The current USDA promotion piece is no longer focused on a pyramid, simply a plate referred to as MyPlate.

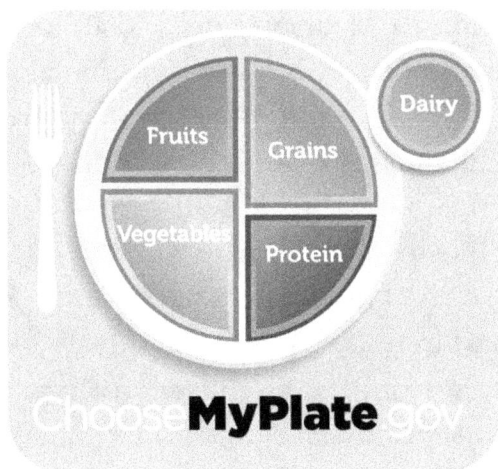

I grew up believing that eating bread was good for you. The government told me so and promoted it. It also told me to drink lots of milk. My parents served bread, in one form or another, and milk every day to our family at just about every meal.

## Not Milk!

Cow's milk, for as long as I can remember, has been promoted as the way to build and maintain strong bones. It is full of vitamin D and calcium, and you should drink at least a glass a day—that is what I was told growing up. There are many studies, however, that question the nutritional value of dairy milk. Some studies have shown that milk drinkers have more frequent bone fractures than those who do not drink milk. Can the calcium found in cow's milk be absorbed by the human body? There are studies that suggest calcium absorption in the human body from milk is minimal[25]. Why milk when a range of leafy vegetables contain a significant amount of calcium that absolutely can be absorbed by humans? What effect does the pasteurization process have on any nutritional aspects of milk? Pasteurization, a process by which milk is heated to kill all forms of microbes and food-borne illnesses, began in the late 1800s. But the pasteurization process kills everything, including many of the nutrients found in milk[26]. While the debate over raw versus pasteurized rages on, the popularity of raw milk appears to be on the rise, as many states now legally allow it to be sold. Raw milk is also found in many of the cheese products you can purchase at your grocery store. On the other hand, consumption of dairy milk is headed in the other direction. Despite this, the dairy milk industry is still big business in the United States, with over $17 billion in sales in 2015[27].

Perhaps the big government food plate should be simplified further, consisting of whole grains, protein, vegetables, and fruits. The cup could go away or be changed from dairy to water. Dairy products such as cheese and yogurt, which are high in protein, could be included in the protein section of the plate.

## Failing the Common-Sense Test

I remember the first time I tried diet soda when I was a kid. The only thing worse than the taste was the aftertaste. I also recall the sales pitch and the reasoning behind drinking diet soda. To summarize, the soda companies took out the refined sugar and replaced it with a synthetic chemical. The result was lower calories, fewer cavities, and better health. For me, however, it failed the common-sense test. How does removing processed sugar and replacing it with a different synthetic chemical, or phony sugar, make it healthier? I never tried diet soda again. I did, however, drink plenty of regular soda growing up and as an adult. Little did I know that the soda industry did not stop at diet soda when it came to replacing refined sugar with a synthetic chemical. In some of the regular soda products, refined sugar was replaced with high-fructose corn syrup (HFCS). HFCS is a sugar substitute made from processed corn. Since the 1950s, corn sweeteners in our diets have increased by eight times. HFCS is cheaper than processed sugar and easy to use[28]. Is there any nutritional value in HFCS? Of course not. Soda is basically made up of water, some type of processed or synthetic sugar, coloring, and other chemicals. Many sodas also contain caffeine, which has its own set of issues. I gave up soda about ten years ago. Until then, I drank it heavily, especially at work. I would drink coffee in the morning and switch to soda in the afternoon. There was an unlimited, free supply of both where I worked, and it was effective for keeping you amped up during the workday. If I stopped drinking it for even a day, however, I would crash hard. And if I didn't have my caffeine fix, I would get headaches. Some also believe caffeine acts as a diuretic, affecting your ability to stay hydrated. As I mention throughout the book, everyone is unique and will be impacted uniquely by different substances, but for me, caffeine often left me feeling less than completely hydrated and lacking energy as the day went on.

## *Phony Food*

Replacing an ingredient in a food or beverage with a synthetic chemical essentially makes it phony. In the case of soda, I'm not sure what you call it when you replace a refined ingredient (sugar) with a synthetic chemical. The government-run system seems to have a tried and tested formula of questioning the nutritional value of a food, which leads to replacing an ingredient, or the entire food product, with a synthetic chemical. In addition to phony sugar, we have phony butter, phony potato chips, phony cream, phony maple syrup, and phony cheese, just to name a few. Some foods have been declared to be high in "bad" cholesterol at one time or another. Cholesterol is a fatlike substance found in all cells in the body. Your body naturally manufactures the cholesterol that is needed to make hormones and substances required to digest food[29]. Cholesterol is also found in the food we eat. Without getting into all the technical details, there is a "good" cholesterol, which carries cholesterol to your liver where it is removed, and a "bad" cholesterol, which builds up in your arteries. The buildup of bad cholesterol is believed to be a major cause of heart disease. Cholesterol can be measured, and if it is viewed as being too high, doctors may recommend a synthetic drug referred to as a statin. If a food was viewed by the government as causing high levels of bad cholesterol, the solution, surprise, was to come up with substitutes for the "bad" ingredients in the form of synthetic chemicals. The public was led to believe these were healthier alternatives. Not only is the natural form of the product healthier in almost all cases, but many of the natural products weren't even unhealthy to begin with, as the government tends to discover some time far off in the future.

Let's look at butter as an example. Butter has a high amount of saturated fat that supposedly raises bad cholesterol. The solution was to replace it with margarine, which is synthetically manufactured and high in trans-fatty acids or trans fat. Margarine gained popularity in the 1980s when studies suggested that eliminating saturated fat from the diet would reduce the risk of heart disease[30]. Recent studies, however, question the link between saturated fat and heart disease[31]. What does not appear to be in question is the link between trans fat and heart disease. Quite ironic if you ask me. Margarine producers will defend their product by stating that the more recent incarnations have replaced the trans fat with other, supposedly healthier ingredients, such as vegetable oils. The problem, once again, is that the vegetable oil is synthetically altered. In this newer version, the process called interesterification alters the molecular structure of the vegetable oil, giving it the properties of fat[32]. Because the process is relatively new, the health ramifications are still being studied and debated. Because there is no definitive proof this process negatively impacts health, don't expect to see the word "interesterification" or any kind of warning show up on a food label. Who do you think loving big government is looking out for anyway? Unfortunately, the track record with synthetic chemicals and food is that the bad news doesn't seem to come out until twenty or so years after the chemical is introduced into the food supply. Having said all of that, I'll stick with butter.

## *Medicine Water*

Speaking of failing the common-sense test, who came up with the idea of adding synthetic chemicals to the water supply? The government, of course, under the guise of preventing tooth decay. Fluoride is added to water in the United States not to improve the quality of the drinking water but as a proactive approach for treating tooth decay. There are a couple problems with medicating the drinking water, the primary one being there is no evidence it prevents tooth decay or reduces cavities. Not only is there no evidence to suggest it works, but many studies show it can cause a great deal of damage[33]. Very few other countries add fluoride to their water. There are more people drinking fluoridated water in the United States, which started adding it to the water in the 1940s, than in the rest of the world combined. Fluoridated drinking water is often portrayed as being derived naturally from phosphorite rock and added to the water supply in such small quantities that health risks are negligible[34]. Further examination shows this justification to be questionable at best. What is added to the water supply is not a natural substance but rather a processed chemical. Silicofluorides is the term for the chemicals used to fluoridate drinking water. They are derived from the industrial manufacturing of phosphate fertilizer[35]. Drinking a synthetic chemical derived from the making of fertilizer is not something that I want my family to sign up for. I involuntarily signed up for it when I was a kid, along with those fluoride treatments at the dentist where you had to bite down on the mouthpiece and try not to gag or swallow the goopy fluoride. I guess my mouthful of fillings shows it did not have much impact. Perhaps better brushing and flossing habits, along with a reduction in sugar intake, would have been a better solution. Studies have shown fluoride exposure can lead to a wide range of health issues including brain damage, arthritis, thyroid disease, dementia, and bone cancer[36]. One study even linked high levels of fluoride found naturally in well water in China to a lower IQ of the children who were drinking it. My family avoids ingesting fluoride by drinking bottled spring water. Unfortunately, many people do not have this option, either because they cannot afford it or they simply don't have ready access to information that would allow them to make an informed decision. Who profits from silicofluoride chemicals? Phosphate-manufacturing companies who sell the chemical to the government with the market size estimated to be as high as $275 million[37].

### Chemical Doused

If you can't add synthetic chemicals to the food or change the chemical composition of the food, you always have the option of dousing it with chemicals. Much of the success of organic foods can be attributed to people being educated about the dangers of the pesticides that are sprayed on the fruits and vegetables they consume. Some pesticides contain heavy metals and toxic chemicals such as arsenic. There are over six hundred chemicals registered for agricultural use in the United States, equating to about sixteen pounds of pesticides applied per person per year[38]. While people respond differently to different chemicals, the idea of eating fruits and vegetables that have been sprayed with toxins, once again, does not pass the common-sense test. The global pesticides business is expected to exceed $80 billion by 2021[39]. While government benefits tremendously from the business, it appears that little is done to check or even determine the health risks associated with ingesting these chemicals. What is also important to understand is that the absorption of various synthetic-chemical pesticides is different for different fruits and vegetables, and so is the amount of pesticide residue that stays on the food. For example, strawberries and peaches are known to contain high amounts of pesticides. The best way to protect your family is to know which fruits and vegetables contain high amounts of pesticides and avoid them by eating organic.

### Chemicals Everywhere

Exposure to synthetic chemicals does not stop with the food and the drugs. Government-sanctioned synthetic chemicals are everywhere. Synthetic chemicals are found in the air, on your lawn, on your furniture, on the carpet, in your shampoo and cosmetics, on the pots and pans you cook with, and on and in many other items that you are exposed to daily. Some chemicals are not as obvious, such as the lining on the inside of many canned goods, which may contain bisphenol A or BPA, a synthetic hormone that has been linked to cancer[40].

In some cases, chemical exposure may make the environment in your home more toxic than the pollution outdoors. With the average home containing about ten gallons of synthetic-chemical products, the Environmental Protection Agency has advised that the average indoor home environment may be twice as toxic as the outdoor environment[41]. The best advice is to not rely totally on your heating and air conditioning units and let some fresh air in your home as much as possible.

## Personal Decisions and Diet Management

Based on experience, research, and an understanding of the synthetic-chemical-based healthcare model in the United States, I have made decisions and changes over the years regarding my own nutritional and health choices. Those changes are primarily focused on reducing my sugar intake. Excessive sugar causes inflammation and, I believe, is a common denominator for almost every major disease that people suffer from today. This is not rocket science, and you don't have to be a genius to figure this out. As Uncle Bob showed me, you also don't need fancy, sophisticated diet programs. Just a little common sense and following a basic formula that you can stick to will lead to improvement.

I quit soda and dramatically reduced my caffeine intake during a vacation, where the impact from the ensuing headaches was minimal. I have had sips of soda here and there over the last ten years, but excluding those exceptions, I live a life that is soda-free. I don't keep soda in my house. My wife occasionally drinks ginger ale. My son mostly sticks to water but will have a soda on occasion. I decided to quit soda only when I made the commitment to make the change a permanent part of my lifestyle. I personally will not make any dietary changes unless I can commit to a permanent change. If I can't stick to it, I won't change it. This philosophy also applies to exercise. If I decide to work out, ride a bike, walk or run, swim, take up yoga, or whatever it may be, I'll start out with something that I can stick to as part of a regular routine and build up from there. Other changes I have made to my personal regimen include the following:

- I don't eat anything but fruit after eight o'clock in the evening. Snacking late at night is not healthy and may adversely impact the quality of your sleep.
- For breakfast, I drink tea and will eat a small amount of fruit or, occasionally, a non-processed protein such as eggs.
- I try to avoid bread or carbs in all forms completely before dinner. For lunch, I will have a salad or some form of non-processed protein or both. Sometimes when I am traveling or am on business, this can be a difficult rule to stick with, but I do my best. If I occasionally break this rule for whatever reason, I strive to immediately come back to it as a routine habit.
- I eat organic as much as possible.
- I don't drink medicated tap water.

There are other opportunities for me to improve my overall wellness through a better diet, but they are changes I know I don't have the willpower to make and stick to permanently. At least not yet. One change would be to further reduce my sugar intake through the complete elimination of desserts and sweets. But I love desserts, so while I know I can commit to skipping them at lunch, I am not ready to completely eliminate them from my diet. Each of us must weigh the anticipated benefit against the cost, and for each of us, the decision is personal.

# CHAPTER 5

# The Druggie Nation

*We are addicted to our thoughts. We cannot change anything if we cannot change our thinking. —Santosh Kalwar, Quote Me Everyday*

The average American spends almost $1,000 a year on synthetic pharmaceutical drugs. This is 40 percent higher than the next highest spender in the world, which happens to be Canada[42]. Close to 50 percent of the American population is taking at least one synthetic drug every month. Over 20 percent are taking three or more a month, and 10 percent are taking five or more per month. Yes, you read that correctly: 10 percent of the population in the United States is on five or more synthetic drugs per month. What is your number? How many synthetic drugs are you on? Physicians prescribed or provided 2.8 billion drugs in the United States in 2013[43]. Let's face it; Americans consume a disproportionate number of synthetic drugs. We live in a country with a system designed to promote and maximize legal (as defined by government) drug use, also maximizing the profits of the pharmaceutical industry and the tax revenue of big government.

### A Witches' Brew

The problem of rampant drug use only increases with age. The average elderly person in the United States, age sixty-five and over, is taking more than five prescription medicines. The average nursing-home patient is taking seven[44]. Between the ages of forty-five and sixty-five, it doesn't get much better, as the average person in that age group is taking four prescription drugs daily[45]. What happens when a person starts mixing drugs? That all depends on the person. Because we each have a unique genetic makeup, we will react differently to different chemical substances. A synthetic drug that may greatly help one person could trigger a range of adverse effects in another.

Even before considering the impact of mixing multiple drugs, a look at the statistics from the Food and Drug Administration (FDA) on adverse reactions to taking any synthetic drug is daunting. In 2014, there were over 800,000 reported adverse events related to pharmaceutical drugs given to people in hospitals with over 120,000 deaths[46]. The total number of adverse reactions to pharmaceutical drugs is estimated at over two million annually. To put this in perspective and appreciate the magnitude of the problem, let's compare the death rate from drug reactions in hospitals to automobile deaths, which generate significantly more publicity. Automobile deaths in the United States numbered 38,300 in 2015, which is roughly a third of the number of deaths related to adverse drug reactions[47]. The pharmaceutical industry provides a warning at the end of its product commercials when it lists the various potential adverse side effects of the drug it is marketing. It is typically a list of items that are rattled off very quickly with the worst items saved for last. But what are the potential negative side effects when you mix two or more synthetic chemicals? Who knows! Has the FDA investigated this? Has it explored all the various combinations of drugs that a person can consume simultaneously? It provides a vague warning on its website, but that is about it. What we do know is that when you start mixing chemicals, you get changed chemicals and potentially different reactions. How a general population reacts to various combinations of chemicals is unknown. How each individual person with a unique genetic makeup reacts to combinations of synthetic chemicals is anyone's guess. What we do know is that the adverse side effects of ingested substances that occur in nature are dramatically lower than those from synthetic drugs[48].

## *Fox Guarding the Henhouse*

The Food and Drug Administration is a federal agency of the US Department of Health and Human Services. Is it a conflict of interest for a group that benefits from the growth and success of the pharmaceutical industry to be the same group in charge of overseeing, regulating, and ensuring that people are informed and protected from it? From the FDA website, the FDA mission is as follows:

> The Food and Drug Administration is responsible for protecting the public health by ensuring the safety, efficacy, and security of human and veterinary drugs, biological products, and medical devices; and by ensuring the safety of our nation's food supply, cosmetics, and products that emit radiation.

> FDA also has responsibility for regulating the manufacturing, marketing, and distribution of tobacco products to protect the public health and to reduce tobacco use by minors. FDA is responsible for advancing the public health by helping to speed innovations that make medical products more effective, safer, and

more affordable and by helping the public get the accurate, science-based information they need to use medical products and foods to maintain and improve their health.

FDA also plays a significant role in the Nation's counterterrorism capability. FDA fulfills this responsibility by ensuring the security of the food supply and by fostering development of medical products to respond to deliberate and naturally emerging public health threats.

The FDA is an independent agency of the federal government, and the people who work in the FDA take their mission and their job very seriously. I want to be clear that the purpose is not to judge the agency specifically or the hard-working, highly competent people who work in it. The goal is to fundamentally understand the system, how it is structured, and the business model that drives it so that we can all better understand what the system produces and why, and make better decisions for ourselves and our families. In the case of the FDA, you would assume that as part of the federal government, it is funded by the taxpayer with the mission (as shown above) to serve the taxpayer. That assumption would be partially false. Congress passed legislation in 1992 called the Prescription Drug User Fee Act (PDUFA) authorizing the FDA to collect fees from companies that produce certain human drug and biological products. And quoting once again from the FDA website, "Since the passage of PDUFA, user fees have played an important role in expediting the drug approval process"[49]. As stated,

the purpose of collecting fees from pharmaceutical companies was to provide more funding for the agency so that the
drug approval process could be accelerated. It is also inter-
esting that passage of this law was driven by complaints from
consumers, the taxpayers, that the approval process for new
synthetic drugs was taking too long. But perhaps that should
not come as a surprise when you have a population that is
preconditioned to accept synthetic pharmaceutical drugs as
the solution to just about every problem. That view is rein-
forced by the continuous bombardment of ads promoting
the benefits of synthetic drugs and the lack of focus on alternatives. In 2010, the pharmaceutical industry paid over
$500 million in fees to the FDA. This covered almost all ex-
penses associated with new drug approval (NDA) reviews[50].

## Miss the Forest for the Trees

Does the FDA spend any time or money exploring substances that occur in nature as alternatives to the synthetic
drugs that it approves and indirectly promotes through that
stamp of approval? Only if those substances are a threat to
public health. In other words, nutraceuticals, defined as any
product derived from food sources with nutritional benefit,
only come to the attention of the FDA if there is some sort of
problem. A good example of this occurred in 2015 when an
FDA investigation resulted in criminal actions against multiple
manufacturers of dietary supplements[51]. While this is appropriate and certainly part of the mission of the FDA, the point
is that the positive aspects of substances that occur in nature,
in the context of alternatives to synthetic drugs, are not part

of the FDA's mission. The warning labels on drug packaging and the warnings at the ends of those television commercials do not include recommendations for alternatives that may not be synthetic and patented. The consumer only sees one option—the synthetic-drug option that is promoted aggressively by powerful and well-funded interest groups along with big government. Alternative natural options are not recommended and require consumers to investigate on their own.

## Gut Check

For a good example of this, let's look at stomach gas or indigestion, sometimes referred to as heartburn. While indigestion may be caused by something simple like eating too fast, it could also be caused by something more serious such as acid reflux disease. Logically, one might think acid reflux is caused by having too much stomach acid. In many cases however, it is just the opposite. The stomach may not produce enough hydrochloric acid (HCL), causing the same symptoms[52]. The cause may also be an overgrowth of bad bacteria in the small intestine and stomach. If either or both are the case, suppressing stomach acid is not going to solve the problem. Despite this, the market for acid-suppressing drugs, also known as proton pump inhibitors, is huge. Over 100 million prescriptions are filled every year for proton pump inhibitors, generating over $13 billion in sales and making this class of synthetic drug the third highest selling in the United States[53]. In addition to reported side effects including fractures and various infections, studies have shown acid-suppressing drugs may limit the body's ability to absorb vitamins and minerals. When consulting a doctor about indigestion symptoms, the course of action in many cases will be to prescribe a drug that will suppress stomach acid. This reflects my personal experience about fifteen years ago when I was dealing with stomach issues and underwent an endoscopy. An endoscopy is a procedure that allows a doctor to see the inside of your esophagus and stomach. Instead of continuing a synthetic-drug regimen, I chose to try something different: probiotics. I believed the solution to my particular problem simply required restoring the balance of good bacteria in the gut, which can be accomplished by taking probiotics and cutting back on carbohydrates (yes, our old friend bread) and sugar. Probiotics have been shown to reduce bacterial overgrowth and address a range of digestive issues[54]. Studies show imbalances in the bacteria or flora found in the gastrointestinal tract, which consists of the stomach and the small and large intestines, may often be the foundational cause of many diseases[55]. Probiotics worked for me, and I continue to take them as a daily supplement. They have also helped my son. One of the decisions my wife and I made when dealing with our son's ADHD was to add probiotics to his daily regimen. His tests showed an intestinal tract imbalance along with a range of food sensitivities. By supplementing his diet with probiotics and other nutrients, we were able to restore balance to his gut and wean him off synthetic drugs.

## A Drug for That

In some cases, diagnostic tests may indicate a risk of disease sometime in the future. The medical establishment has come up with a "predisease" category in which measured indicators suggest you may be heading toward a disease state but are not quite there yet. This is an effective way of extending the definition of a disease to include individuals who are not presently showing symptoms of a disease[56]. And it logically follows that if you can extend how a disease is defined, you can also extend the market opportunity for synthetic drugs. Examples of predisease conditions include prediabetes and prehypertension or pre-high blood pressure. While doctors will almost always recommend changes in diet or lifestyle for patients in the predisease category, they may also supplement the recommendation with synthetic drugs.

Taking this logic even further, recommending small, daily doses of aspirin to older patients has become popular as a general supplement to prevent future cardiovascular issues. Recent studies, however, have once again shown that the side effects, such as stomach bleeding, may outweigh any perceived health benefit[57].

### *Vital Signs*

It is important to state that measured indicators of the body's health known as vital signs can be tracked and should be taken very seriously if they are trending in the wrong direction. Vital sign measurements include body temperature, pulse rate, respiration rate, and blood pressure[58]. Vital signs can be measured and tracked when you visit a doctor or by yourself at home. Your blood pressure measurement is particularly important. When your blood pressure is measured, two numbers are recorded. One measures the pressure in your artery when the heart is pumping blood. The other measures the pressure in the artery when the heart is at rest. A blood pressure reading that is considered normal or healthy may be different for everyone, because once again, we all have a different genetic makeup. Each individual blood pressure measurement may also vary based on a wide range of factors that occur in everyday life. What is important is the medium- to longer-term trend. If blood pressure is rising or falling at an unacceptable rate over time, it could indicate a potentially serious health problem. My dad was diagnosed with high blood pressure, or hypertension, in his forties. I am not saying there was a correlation to his cancer, but it was certainly a red flag and an indicator that something was not right.

As many as one-third of American adults may have high blood pressure, which, of course, makes hypertension a huge market for a wide range of synthetic drugs. When my dad was diagnosed with high blood pressure, salt was considered the enemy. If you had elevated blood pressure like my dad at the time, you were given hypertension drugs and put on a low-salt diet. I was taught as a kid that salt was bad, and it should not be added to food. Time has shown once again that, while too much of anything is probably bad for you, salt is not the bogeyman that it was made out to be in my youth. As a matter of fact, salt is a naturally occurring substance that your body requires to maintain good health. Recent studies dispute the data that links salt intake to high blood pressure and suggests that low salt intake may increase the risk of certain diseases[59]. While synthetic drugs may be required to treat certain cases of hypertension, a change of lifestyle that includes diet and exercise should be investigated and strongly considered to at least augment any synthetic-drug regimen. The questions that should always be asked are the same questions that I asked when my son was diagnosed ADHD and prescribed drugs: what is the underlying cause, what steps can I take to impact the cause in a positive way that don't involve synthetic chemicals, and how long will I need to be on the drug? If you do not get an answer from the establishment to the last question, you can assume the answer is forever. With a few exceptions, being on a synthetic drug forever is not what I would consider an acceptable solution, unless of course you happen to be a pharmaceutical company or the government.

One measurement that is not considered a vital sign but is also worth mentioning as an important indicator of overall health and fitness, including potential problems if it trends in the wrong direction, is blood oxygen level. Blood oxygen level is a measurement of the amount of oxygen available in the blood and should be in the 90 to 100 percent range in healthy individuals[60]. Blood oxygen can easily be measured with a device called a pulse oximeter, or pulse ox for short, that attaches to the end of your fingertip.

### Pain Check

The most egregious example of prescription drugs gone wild can be found in the opioid epidemic. Allow me to tell you a story that I have heard way too often in the United States. A young person plays a particular sport in high school or college. He or she suffers an injury. As part of the treatment of said injury, the person is given a prescription pain-killer known as an opioid. These painkillers are highly addictive but very profitable for the pharmaceutical industry, medical establishment, and government that jointly profit from them. The young person becomes addicted. Unable to kick the addiction over time, he or she graduates to a higher form of opioid such as heroin. Unable to kick that addiction, he or she overdoses and dies.

The prescription drug market for opioids in the United States is close to $10 billion with nearly 249 million prescriptions in 2015. That is more than double the amount that was prescribed in 1992. While opioids certainly have a proper role in relieving suffering and pain in end-of-life situations, the addictive nature of the drug combined with the frequency of which it is prescribed should have sounded alarms a long time ago. Instead of sounding alarms, however, and clamping down on the doctors who prescribe opioids like candy, one solution amazingly is just to create more drugs to treat the various symptoms generated by the opioids themselves. These symptoms range from constipation to insomnia to the very dependency or addiction created by the opioid drug. The market for drugs that treat symptoms of opioid prescription drugs is estimated to be greater than $5 billion[61]. I find it staggering that in the United States of America, you could have a drug market of over $5 billion specifically focused on dealing with the side effects generated from another drug that is clearly being overprescribed and killing people.

Research is showing that abuse of prescription painkillers is the gateway to heroin use and addiction. Nearly half of young people who injected heroin reported previously using prescription opioids before starting on heroin. Heroin being cheaper and easier to obtain was cited as the reason for the switch[62]. Opioid abuse in the form of prescription drugs and heroin is causing death in this country on a scale never seen before with any other drug. In 2014, 47,055 drug overdose deaths occurred in the United States. Of those deaths, 61 percent were caused by some type of opioid. Heroin overdoses have more than tripled in the last four years[63]. What is tragic is the large numbers of young people included in these statistics. This is an epidemic rooted in the overprescription of pharmaceutical opioids. Anything else that would cause this level of destruction to the younger generation of Americans would spark a national outcry and emergency. But the solution to the problem is the same as the solution to so many other problems—create more synthetic drugs. I can think of no better example that illustrates how broken our synthetic-drug-based system and culture has become than the opioid epidemic.

### Needle Me

Perhaps the cycle described in the opioid story could be short-circuited if the medical establishment and its enablers in big government were more proactive in recommending alternatives to opioid medications. But once again, it appears that natural alternatives are rarely introduced as viable options. You either put your faith in the medical establishment, or you figure it out for yourself. One alternative I use for relieving many different types of pain is acupuncture. Acupuncture is a form of treatment that began in China over twenty-five hundred years ago. It is focused on stimulating the body by inserting needles into specific points. The needles create a flow of energy called qi (pronounced "chee") from the various points through pathways in the body. Improving the flow of energy reduces pain and leads to improved health. Studies have shown that acupuncture has been effective in treating a range of diseases, including opioid addiction. Acupuncture appears to stimulate neurons in the brain in such a way as to release a brain chemical called dopamine, which reduces the effects of positive and negative reinforcement in opioid addiction. I have personally relied on acupuncture treatments to successfully address a range of issues including back and neck pain. Natural alternatives may provide a step in the right direction to address the opioid epidemic along with numerous other health issues. Now we only need to change the system so that more people can benefit from these options.

### *Get Your Flu Shot Here*

Is there anything more hyped than the flu shot? It used to be that the flu, or influenza, vaccine was given only to the elderly who had weakened immune systems and were susceptible to complications, such as pneumonia, that could be triggered by the virus. Now the flu shot is the greatest thing since sliced bread, and everyone must have it. You can get it anywhere, at the doctor's office, the pharmacy, and even the grocery store. The promotion of the flu shot is continuous on all forms of media. And if you choose not to get the flu shot, you might lose your job, or your child may not be able to attend school. Why all the hype? What exactly is in a flu shot? Besides the various strains of the vaccine, which change yearly depending on the type of flu being targeted, ingredients in the vaccine may include items such as formaldehyde, aluminum salts, gelatin, antibiotics, chicken egg proteins, and thimerosal, which contains a form of mercury[64]. The global market for the flu vaccine exceeds $3 billion, with the United States, of course, being the largest market[65]. The flu shot is now recommended by the government for every American over the age of six months. If you work in a hospital, an annual flu shot is a condition of employment. Does the flu shot even work? That depends on who you ask. Some studies show the impact of the shot to be modest at best[66]. The Centers for Disease Control and Prevention (CDC) even admits that the effectiveness of the vaccine can vary from season to season and person to person. It estimates that the vaccine can reduce the risk of the flu by 50 to 60 percent, whatever that means. The flu shot has also been shown to have side effects, and additional concerns have been raised regarding effectiveness when the shot is taken in combination with other drugs. The metric that the CDC cites as a benchmark to champion the need for the vaccine is "estimated number of deaths" caused by the virus, although the actual number of deaths caused by influenza is not reported or tracked[67]. CDC estimates of deaths caused by influenza range from three thousand to fifty-six thousand annually. But if deaths caused by influenza are not tracked, how do we really know if the vaccine is having a positive impact or not? I guess we just need to trust the medical establishment. I'll take a pass on that along with the flu shot.

# CHAPTER 6

# The Scourge of Cancer

*We cannot know the whole truth, which belongs to God alone, but our task nevertheless is to seek to know what is true. And if we offend gravely enough against what we know to be true, as by failing badly enough to deal affectionately and responsibly with our land and our neighbors, truth will retaliate with ugliness, poverty, and disease. —Wendell Berry*

Cancer is big business! The global market for cancer drugs exceeds $100 billion annually[68]. If you factor in all costs associated with insurance, treatment, support, capital equipment, and care at various stages of the disease, the overall market may easily be double. In addition to being big business, it is also a deadly business. It is estimated, in 2017, over 1.6 million people in the United States will be diagnosed with cancer, and over 600,000 will die of the disease[69]. Let's take a closer look at cancer, the disease that has caused pain, suffering, and death to my family and millions of others worldwide.

## What Is Cancer?

I recall my early conversations in the mid-1980s with Uncle Bob after I found out my dad was diagnosed with cancer. One of the first questions he asked me was—does anyone even know what cancer is and what causes it? The question was clearly rhetorical, as in his opinion, the answer was a resounding no. After pondering this question for several days and doing my own research, I found myself agreeing with Uncle Bob. So, what is cancer, and what causes it? Is it something you inherit, and it just manifests itself at some point in life? Is it a genetic problem? Is it a virus? Is it something you get from smoking or being exposed to pesticides? And if we aren't clear on what cancer is, how could we possibly expect to effectively treat it or cure it? As an engineer,

I was taught that if you can't fundamentally understand the nature of a problem, you will never be able to solve it.

Let's fast forward to today, 2017, and ask again—what is cancer, and what is the underlying cause? When you conduct some research, you find that there are many different types of cancers (over one hundred) with many different explanations for causes. The technical answer that you find consistently is that cancer is defined as abnormal cells dividing uncontrollably and spreading into surrounding tissue[70]. But is that a fundamental definition of what cancer is or simply how cancer manifests itself? The National Cancer Institute states that cancer is a "genetic disease" that can be inherited from parents or triggered over one's lifetime from a range of "environmental exposures." The American Cancer Society claims viruses can cause certain types of cancer[71]. A virus is a small, infectious agent that requires the assistance of a living host to survive and replicate[72]. You can catch a virus, so can you catch cancer? Apparently, you can from specific viruses such as human papilloma virus (HPV), which can cause cervical cancer. Bacteria can also cause cancer, according to the American Cancer Society, with stomach cancer being an example. Finally, microbes and parasites in the vital organs are sometimes noted as potential causes of a range of cancers. Based on this knowledge, one could conclude that depending on the type of cancer you have, the cause could potentially be several different sources or factors. There are also numerous alternative theories on what causes cancer, including microbes or bacteria that enter a cell and cause low ATP (adenosine triphosphate) energy, which results in the cells becoming cancerous[73]. This still does not provide a fundamental explanation of what cancer is. If at this point you are thoroughly confused, welcome to my world, and consider the possibility that confusion may be the objective. When a subject is complex and confusing, the inclination seems to be to rely on the medical establishment and "experts" to deal with it.

## *Hope It Sticks*

When a disease is defined in such broad terms as "bad cells multiplying out of control" and there are over one hundred manifestations of the disease, and you have a multiple choice of causes, what do you do? You make a lot of money, and the pharmaceutical industry, along with its enablers and partners in big government, has been extremely successful in this respect over the last fifty years. According to the National Cancer Institute, there are more than two hundred pharmaceutical drugs for treating cancer[74]. But you don't necessarily have to take a drug to treat cancer. You can opt for surgery, radiation, or a combination of these with the drugs. Do any of these drugs, or the drugs combined with surgery or radiation, cure cancer? They are used to treat cancer and are described as "treatments." They may kill cancer cells, they may slow down the spread of cancer, they may stop the cancer cells from multiplying, but do they eradicate the disease? Do they solve the underlying problem such in a way that you can confidently be assured that it won't return? The answer to these questions appears to be no. The approach is clearly to cut it, burn it, poison it, but not cure it. The drugs and treatments are focused on the symptoms of specific types of cancer, and the process for creating these drugs and the hoped-for results are akin to throwing something against a wall and hoping it sticks. Most cancer drugs fall into a category referred to as chemotherapy. The purpose of chemotherapy is to kill cancer cells. The problems however, are many. Let's start with the fact that chemotherapy drugs are toxic and kill more than just cancer cells; they kill all cells. And then you have the side effects, which, depending on several factors including your genetic makeup, could include nausea, hair loss, infection, bleeding, kidney damage, nervous system damage, memory loss, and a whole host of other things including death. Some of these side effects can be addressed by, you guessed it, additional drugs. If a company can develop a synthetic drug that will treat cancer by killing cancer cells for a specific type of cancer, it can patent it and make tons of money. So it develops and tests various chemical combinations looking for that combination that will stick, not in the context of establishing a fundamental understanding of the very nature of cancer and coming up with an innovative solution to solve it, but simply to poison and kill some cancer cells.

### Alternative Cancer Solutions

In our synthetic-drug-centric model that is pushed by the medical establishment and big government, substances that occur in nature and natural treatments get shortchanged. The medical establishment does not promote these solutions, and in many cases, they are discouraged and frowned upon. Discovering alternatives requires you to research and investigate. While there are plenty of websites, alternative newsletters, alternative treatments, and so on, there is no guidebook that organizes them based on your or your loved one's specific condition. Some of the information may be misleading or inaccurate. There is no filter to inform you of hoaxes and treatments that may not be effective. The government only focuses on synthetic drugs and only investigates natural products when something clearly goes wrong. In dealing with cancer, there are many natural alternatives that are based on bolstering the body's environment and immune system so that it can cure itself and maintain a healthy state, but you must do the legwork and decide what is best for you.

## Bad Acid

During one of my visits with Uncle Bob at a Las Vegas buffet, we were engaged in one of our many discussions on approaches for dealing with cancer. Uncle Bob, after his initial diagnoses of heart issues years earlier and a round with cancer, had a very strict vegetarian diet, and he did not eat any type of meat. At some point in the conversation, Uncle Bob pointed to a slice of prime rib sitting on my plate and commented, "If your doctor were to tell you that if you eat that, you will die, I'd bet that you would stop eating now." He went on further to explain that cancer creates and thrives in an acidic environment and that meat and other acidic foods can facilitate the creation of such an environment. Foods such as meat and sugar create an acidic environment in your gut, as they are more difficult to digest. Alkaline foods, such as fruits and vegetables, have the opposite effect, creating good bacteria and reducing inflammation. As discussed earlier, maintaining good gut health is key to preventing disease. Toxins are also acidic, and as we age and more toxins are absorbed by the body, our system becomes more acidic. While increasing the pH of your body to a level that is more alkaline will not cure cancer, a diet that recognizes the acidic and alkaline nature of various foods and promotes the alkaline will reduce inflammation and may help the body in preventing cancer and other diseases.

## *Super C*

Vitamin C, also known as ascorbic acid, is a powerful antioxidant found in many of the foods that my family enjoys, including oranges, strawberries, peppers, and broccoli. It helps the body form and maintain tissue, which includes bones, skin, and blood vessels. My family takes vitamin C daily as a nutritional supplement. In the cold and flu seasons, we increase the dose. Recently, vitamin C has received publicity as a potential treatment for various types of cancer. High doses of vitamin C given intravenously have been shown to slow the growth and spread of many cancers with minimal side effects, according to the National Cancer Institute[75]. This is quite an admission coming from the government. Vitamin C has always been known to supercharge the body's immune system, but taken intravenously, vitamin C increases the production of hydrogen peroxide, which targets and eradicates cancer cells in the body[76]. Intravenous vitamin C appears to be gaining momentum as an alternative treatment for cancer.

## *Common Denominators*

While there may not be a magic synthetic pill to cure cancer, there is a common formula that may help reduce the odds of getting cancer and many other diseases. It is based on minimizing the negative substances we are exposed to and maximizing the positive. The negative items are:

- Sugar and substances that create sugar with the primary villain being carbs, or the "bread" category, as I like to refer to it, and starches
- Overreliance on synthetic drugs
- Acidic foods in large quantities at the expense of alkaline foods
- Toxins, which may include pesticides and heavy metals
- Synthetic chemicals in food, such as trans-fatty acids and those found in diet soda
- Excessive stress and fatigue

The positive are:

- Fruits and vegetables, especially those that lean toward the alkaline side of the scale
- Substances that promote good gut health like probiotics
- Nonsynthetic vitamin supplements with an emphasis on vitamin C and other antioxidants
- Clean, nonmedicated water and air
- Moderate exercise

With regard to solving the riddle known as cancer, I have hope and believe the future is bright. My hope and faith, however, do not sit with the synthetic-chemical-based establishment and its big government partner but with an emerging industry, new technology, and a new paradigm for healthcare that we'll discuss shortly.

# CHAPTER 7

# The Puppet Master

*America is the greatest engine of innovation that has ever existed, and it can't be duplicated anytime soon, because it is the product of a multitude of factors: extreme freedom of thought, an emphasis on independent thinking, a steady immigration of new minds, a risk-taking culture with no stigma attached to trying and failing, a noncorrupt bureaucracy, and financial markets and a venture capital system that are unrivaled at taking new ideas and turning them into global products.*
*—Thomas L. Friedman*

Oh, those horrible big business capitalists. You hear it all the time. The evil corporations who only care about making money, and on the other side, loving big government with its noble intentions working to protect us and make the world better, keeping the evildoers in check through taxes, laws, programs, and regulations. This is the view promoted by some who call for bigger government, and it is often rooted in a fundamental lack of understanding of how wealth and the standard of living of a society is generated and what drives private companies and big government.

## *Economics 101*

It is true that companies in the private sector are driven by growth in revenue and profit, the metrics from which they are measured by their investors and shareholders who risk their capital when they invest. For a private company to grow and profit, the company must bring to market, in an efficient manner, a product or service for which the market has a need. If the market, which is comprised of consumers, businesses, government, and nonprofit organizations, rejects the product or service, then the company does not generate sufficient revenue to cover its costs and make a profit. The market, collectively, is the ultimate judge of the product, service, and company in a true capitalist system. Private-sector companies that do not return profits to their investors eventually go out of business. Companies that fail to continuously innovate and deliver new value to their customers, even if they were successful in the past, risk being displaced. The opportunity to create new wealth encourages competition and filling any voids that may exist in the market. Failure to innovate can result in the fortunes of any company being reversed, with acquisition or bankruptcy being possible outcomes. Times change, and so do the requirements, expectations, and tastes of customers that make up the marketplace. Well-executed new ideas and business models create enormous amounts of wealth, jobs, profits for investors, and tax revenue for government. There are countless examples over time of companies that failed to innovate and were eventually displaced. And in many cases, innovation results in entire industries being displaced. This process, known as creative destruction, is the cornerstone of the capitalist model[77].

## Government Drivers

The government, or public sector, consists of government, government employees, and the ecosystem that supports and sustains it. There is no free market or market mechanism to determine the effectiveness or the level of demand, if any, for the goods and services produced by government. Budgets are created annually for government departments, with the primary goal of spending all the money in the budget so that the budget will be maintained or increased in the following year. The underlying driver in the public sector is spending. How could you ask for a larger budget if you did not spend all the money in the previous year?

The competition is other departments or agencies that also want to increase their budgets. Are there incentives to be innovative, productive, or efficient? There are no investors, just politicians, lawyers, and taxpayers. The federal government's system of baseline budgeting legislates that spending from a previous year be carried over and be treated as a "floor" for spending in the ensuing year. The spending floor is adjusted upward based on several factors that essentially make it impossible for our federal government to ever truly cut spending. The debate is only over how much spending will be increased and what departments will reap an outsized portion of the increase. If government is not effective, cuts to spending or outright elimination of departments or programs is never a serious consideration. Government politicians simply raise taxes or add to the debt, to be paid off someday by your children and grandchildren long after the politicians are comfortably retired.

## Crony Capitalism

It is the very nature of the two systems that makes a free market system, and the private sector, a more effective and efficient allocator of capital when compared to big government. In the private sector, capital naturally flows to where it will be effectively allocated—companies that are growing, innovative, and profitable. In government, capital is extracted from private individuals and businesses in the form of taxes and fees and used to maintain and grow a bureaucracy. In government, capital gravitates toward political power. When economic growth does not keep up with government growth, the result is deficits and increasing debt. Unsustainable government debt impedes private markets, and as debt accumulates, it becomes harder for the economy to grow at a healthy rate. At some point, economic policies must enable accelerated private-sector growth, the government must cut spending, or some combination of both. Ultimately, the private sector produces an outsized proportion of the wealth that generates the tax revenue that funds the government that pays the salaries and benefits of government workers in addition to services and entitlements received by citizens. Problems occur when you start mixing various facets of these two systems and when big government and private industry actively and cooperatively engage to influence and control components of the other, to the benefit of both parties but perhaps not to the benefit of the customer or citizen. When relationships between government and industry determine success, at the expense of the requirements and well-being of the free market and its customers, the economy and the citizens who depend on the health of the economy will suffer. In my view, the symbiotic relationship between big government and the synthetic-chemical industry has created a system that primarily benefits themselves, with benefit to citizens and customers they both profess to serve being a secondary consideration. This type of relationship is often referred to as crony capitalism, but it is better described as a partnership between the manufacturers of synthetic drugs and chemicals and the government. The partnership is designed to maintain a system that promotes the sale of synthetic chemicals above all other alternatives and ensures that the profits of synthetic-chemical manufacturers are optimized. And let's be clear; while industry tends to be on the receiving end of the negative publicity in these relationships, it is the government and the politicians that hold disproportional power and call the shots, not the other way around. The government sets the rules of engagement and is the master in this partnership with the ability to alter the system and change the rules at any time and for any reason, whether good or bad.

## *Politicization*

The role of government is to create a fair system, a level playing field that does not favor one group over another, with laws that are enforced and are in the best interest of the citizens of the country. When government creates rules or regulations that benefit one party over another, or becomes an active participant in the system, the system often becomes inefficient and imbalanced. In some cases, a system, a program, or even government research may become politicized to increase the power and size of government. Longer-term, higher-risk research and development is a good example, in my view, where not being exposed to short- and medium-term profit demands of the marketplace is an advantage, and government investment can enable technological progress and augment the private market. Government research and development that resulted in the Internet serves as a great example. We'll discuss another that is critical to the future of healthcare in the next chapter. On the other hand, government-sponsored research into global warming or climate change provides a more politicized example. The debate is not over whether our climate is changing. The debate centers on the specific, quantifiable impact of humans on that change and what is going to be done about it. The government solution is always the same regardless of the problem: bigger government. Regulations need to be created, carbon emitters need to be taxed, a bureaucracy needs to be built to ensure the rules are followed, and so on and so on. If you advocate for bigger government, you must assume that government is capable of effectively addressing and solving the targeted problem. Often, noble intentions of big government are confused with actual performance and results. Costs are rarely an issue or concern. Big government and the politicians that run it believe they know best and care more, so they should be calling the shots. This is simply a form of arrogance disguised as nobility. Have you ever heard of a proposed solution to the global warming concerns that does not involve a bigger role and more power for government? I would personally support any global warming initiative that does not include any incremental big government spending, any additional big government headcount adds, and any additional confiscation of wealth through taxation of the productive part of the economy, and that would be the private sector. I won't hold my breath.

The change of a few degrees in temperature caused by humans and the burning of fossil fuels could ultimately wipe out the planet someday; I get it. But what about the devastating consequences that are being inflicted today on a society hooked on synthetic chemicals? Why is one in the news constantly while the other barely shows up on the radar? The reason is simple. Global warming research has the potential to create a new opportunity and ecosystem to extend the reach and power of big government, while synthetic chemicals are already a mature, booming business where the goal is simply to maintain, and not disturb, the status quo.

## Big Government Immersion

When you examine the pharmaceutical industry supply chain and business model, you find the government everywhere. From establishing and managing the system for approving and patenting new drugs, to driving new drug research and development of which government provides roughly a third of the funding, to enabling the aggressive promotion and advertising of synthetic drugs, big government plays a critical role in ensuring the viability of the pharmaceutical industry. Big pharma returns the favor through political contributions, taxes, and also fees, as discussed earlier, to fund the various agencies responsible for regulating them. In my opinion, both are also committed to ensuring that any insurance system further reinforces the pharmaceutical industry's position of providing synthetic drugs as the first line of defense for almost all medical conditions. I have yet to visit a doctor who would recommend chiropractic for relief of back pain or acupuncture for anxiety and insomnia. My insurance doesn't even cover these treatments, and it provides little financial incentive to maintain a healthy lifestyle.

## New Customers and the ACA

The Affordable Care Act (ACA) is a great example of the government ingratiating new customers to the wonders of synthetic drugs. I recently left a job and started my own consulting practice, which required that I go out and purchase health insurance for my family. In the last fifteen years, I was similarly required to do this on two other occasions. My most recent experience was not pleasant. In the state where I reside, there were few insurance providers on Healthcare.gov that were still participating in the ACA. The minimum bronze plan that I could purchase for a family of three was over $1000 a month. This was roughly double what I paid the last time I had to search for a plan six years ago. And for the pleasure of paying that every month, I would get deductibles and out-of-pocket maximums that exceeded $10,000. What a deal! With private insurance, outside of the government-controlled ACA plan, I found that I had many options at prices that were a fraction of the ACA price and provided some value without having to reach an insane deductible.

What exactly is the goal of the ACA? If you go to the Healthcare.gov website, you find its stated goals are as follows:

1) Make affordable health insurance available to more people with an emphasis on those who may not be able to presently afford it.
2) Expand Medicaid to cover all adults with income below 138 percent of the poverty level.
3) Lower the costs of healthcare[78].

When examining these goals, the first thing that jumps out is the apparent overlap between goals number one and two. Medicaid is a federal program to provide healthcare for low-income, financially needy people, set up by the federal government and administered differently in each state[79]. Wouldn't expanding Medicaid increase the access to healthcare for more people? The US Supreme Court rejected the provision of the ACA that forced states to expand Medicaid, effectively making it optional. The states that have chosen to expand it have seen sharp decreases in their uninsured rates[80]. This essentially answers my question and illustrates that the first two items are different options for accomplishing the same goal. The problem is the third goal. If you expand access to the existing synthetic-drug-centric healthcare system but fail to fundamentally transform the system to make it more effective and efficient with reduced costs, what happens? It is estimated the Medicaid expansion covers nine to ten million people at a cost of $6,336 per person in 2015, which is about 49 percent higher than what was estimated[81]. In states that don't have the expanded Medicaid program, costs to the hospitals that provide medical services are higher, as many bills go unpaid. Those costs get passed on to citizens in the form of higher costs, higher taxes, or higher private insurance rates. For the states that did expand the program, the federal government, whose debt has roughly doubled in the last eight years, reimburses the states for the complete cost of the expansion through 2016. Beginning in 2017, the states must pick up a portion of the costs up to a maximum of 10 percent by 2020. The difference between the states and the federal government is that the states don't have money-printing machines in their basements. State constitutions and statutes require that they balance their budgets (with Vermont being an exception) on a yearly basis. This makes the combination of increased healthcare costs along with that miniscule additional 10 percent for expanded Medicaid potentially toxic for their budgets. What the ACA is proving is that if you can't control costs, the system will implode. The health exchanges that were created to provide affordable health insurance to more people are falling apart as the health insurance companies pull out of the program and the customers show little interest in the overpriced product that provides little more than catastrophic coverage. In a captive market where the government forces you to purchase a product, it is stunning to realize that the party who appears to be the obvious beneficiary of the scheme, the insurance companies, are pulling out because they can't make money.

The problem with healthcare in the United States has nothing to do with insurance. If you have an issue with insurance companies, simply relax the regulations to allow them to compete across state lines. The increased level of competition will address issues related to insurance cost and plan options. The real issue is the out-of-control cost of healthcare and the broken system that enables it. The politicization of the debate over healthcare has also been frustrating. One example is how the statement "access to healthcare" has been twisted and manipulated to support false narratives that drove passage of the ACA. The perception in the minds of some, including myself for some time, was poor families and their children had no access to healthcare whatsoever. The truth is many had a form of access; they just didn't have insurance. Their level of access was limited and delivered in the costliest form possible, which would be the hospital. All hospitals are bound by law to accept all patients in emergency situations, regardless of their ability to pay. Public hospitals and nonprofit hospitals also must accept low-income patients and waive or subsidize costs, even in nonemergency situations[82]. This effectively turned the hospital into the doctor's office for low-income patients. By increasing the numbers of insured among those with lower income, the number of expensive hospital visits would decrease, and costs would come down. That was the theory anyway, but like many noble government intrusions into the economy, it hasn't worked out that way, as costs continue to skyrocket along with big government debt. US healthcare costs have increased from $27.2 billion in 1960, which equals 5 percent of gross domestic product (GDP), to $3.2 trillion in 2015, equaling 17.8 percent of GDP[83]. Over $1 trillion of that increase has come in the last ten years. The accelerated increase in costs over the last ten years along with the associated debt burden has acted as an anchor on the economy, resulting in anemic economic growth coming out of the 2008 and 2009 recession. Unless you subscribe to the theory that money grows on trees or is generated in unlimited quantities from government basements, this does not end well. Without cost containment, the implosion of the ACA was predictable; the only question was one of timing. The same could be said of the financial health of the US government.

According to the Department of Health and Human Services (HHS), the ACA has enabled 17.7 million new people to purchase health insurance since 2013[84]. For many of these people, their new ACA insurance is subsidized. This is great news for the pharmaceutical industry, as it now has many new customers pulled into a system, subsidized by big government, who will purchase and consume more of its products. The underlying system, however, apart from adding more government bureaucracy, did not change, and the costs continue to rise unchecked. The big government puppet master either has no interest in transforming a broken system or simply doesn't know how. It does, however, know how to add new customers and create new opportunities to sell more synthetic chemicals. This is how you keep the cronies happy and the synthetic-chemical gravy train rolling.

# CHAPTER 8

# A New Way

---

*And it ought to be remembered that there is nothing more difficult to take in hand, more perilous to conduct, or more uncertain in its success, than to take the lead in the introduction of a new order of things. Because the innovator has for enemies all those who have done well under the old conditions, and lukewarm defenders in those who may do well under the new. This coolness arises partly from fear of the opponents, who have the laws on their side, and partly from the incredulity of men, who do not readily believe in new things until they have had a long experience of them. —Niccolò Machiavelli, The Prince*

The world of healthcare is in the early stages of a major transformation. The seismic shift, like many that have occurred in the past, is being driven by new ideas and technology. Major advances in computing and software technology, along with an emerging technology, genomics, are enabling innovative new approaches and providing hope for the future. Genomics is the study of human genes and chromosomes[85]. Genomics sprang out of a government research project and has the potential to drive a new wellness and healthcare model that will be tailored or customized to each individual based on the person's genetic makeup and how he or she reacts and responds to chemical substances, regardless of whether they occur in nature or are created synthetically. A genetic-centric wellness model will be a major shift from the synthetic-chemical-centric treatment model that has been in place for the last fifty-plus years.

## *The Human Genome Project*

The Human Genome Project is a government research project that began in 1988 with the goal of identifying and mapping all the genes in the human body. Even though, as human beings, over 99 percent of our genetic makeup or "genome" is the same, everyone on the planet is unique. It is that less than 1 percent that makes each of us unique and contains the variables that make us look different, feel different, and react differently to our environment. The technical definition of genome is the genetic material contained in your twenty-three pairs of chromosomes (forty-six total), which consist of more than twenty thousand genes[86]. Of the twenty-three pairs of chromosomes, twenty-two are the same for men and women. The twenty-third chromosome determines the sex, with women having two X chromosomes, while men have one X and one Y. The genetic material, or genes, is made up of deoxyribonucleic acid, or DNA, which is the double-helix-shaped molecule residing in a cell's nucleus. DNA molecules are made up of two paired strands, which are derived from a combination of four chemical units called nucleotide bases. The pairing up of these bases in a sequence is what makes up the human genome[87]. How these DNA molecules are sequenced or arranged determines the specific gene and the trait associated with the gene. An example of a trait would be the shape and size of your nose or color of your eyes. To summarize, the specific sequence of multiple DNA molecules makes up a gene, and genes make up chromosomes, which are in the nucleus of each of our cells. Our bodies are made up of millions of cells, and the total combination of sequenced nucleotide base pairs is 3.2 billion[88]. The Human Genome Project was an attempt to create a map of the genetic makeup of the human body. Creating that map was a herculean task when you consider that it required identifying and properly sorting a staggering number of variables.

In 2003, the map of the human genome was published. The map covers over 90 percent of the human genome and was made available over the Internet for private or public individuals or companies to leverage for research or the development of new healthcare treatments. The Human

Genome Project is a great example of pure research and development with clearly defined goals and objectives. The cost to the taxpayer was less than $3 billion. This figure should prove over time to be a great investment in the context of the future benefit to society and a new industry that is already emerging from this research. This industry has the potential to create incredible amounts of wealth, jobs, and a new paradigm for wellness and healthcare.

### *Complexity and Computing Power*

When examining the complexity associated with mapping humans genetically, the Human Genome Project was just a starting point. The published results of the project provide a high-level map of the human body. As you get into more specifics, you begin to appreciate the enormous number of variables that impact health and the challenge in leveraging those variables to create solutions. The genome generated by the Human Genome Project was based on DNA samples from several unidentified volunteers. Creating a genomic sequence for each unique individual is not only more challenging but, for it to be useful, requires additional data and analysis. What makes a person unique goes beyond the sequencing of DNA in genes. Variants or different versions of the same genes, mutations in genes, the length of genes, and DNA that exists outside of genes (which is where 98.5 percent of our DNA resides) all impact our own unique makeup. And the variables change over time. From a computing technology standpoint, the ability to absorb and analyze these variables would have been unimaginable even at the turn of the century when the Human Genome Project was wrapping up. Today, that is no longer the case. You have more computing power in your smartphone then NASA had in all its computers when it sent a man to the moon in 1969[89]. It is estimated that we have experienced a trillionfold increase in computing power over the last sixty years. Moore's Law states that computing processing power doubles every two years[90]. This continuous increase in computing technology and power is driving major advances in data analytics, artificial intelligence, and machine-learning software. The combination of advanced computing power, the Internet, and new analytics and collaboration software is driving step changes in discovery and knowledge through the ability to analyze and share large amounts of data and collaborate on projects regardless of physical location. The combination of all these factors is bringing us rapidly closer to the realization of ideas that many of us thought were science fiction and would not expect to witness in our lifetime. These ideas span many different industries and include widely publicized concepts like autonomous (self-driving) vehicles and even personal autonomous vehicles that fly. Though it may receive less fanfare and glitz, these advances in technology are also having a major impact on genetic engineering.

## Modern Genetic Testing

Today, you can send out a saliva sample containing your DNA and, in a few weeks, receive a complete report on your genetic makeup. That report will include tendencies toward specific diseases and how your body may react to certain synthetic drugs. Companies are now testing for markers that even determine genetic physical and learning characteristics, pointing you to identify and invest in areas where you may have potential and talent. As time marches on and the technology improves, the accuracy of the testing and the associated recommendations will improve, and the functional capabilities will expand. While this is exciting, the real opportunity lies in using one's unique genome to optimize health, wellness, and treatment programs.

## A New Era for Healthcare

We are entering an era where your personal genome may provide the foundation for a transformative new healthcare model. In this model, your unique genetic makeup, combined with vital signs and other health-related measurements, will drive a range of programs tailored to your needs. These programs will include specific exercise and diet regimen recommendations, which will be based not only on sensitivities and what substances impact you in positive and negative ways, but also on your own personal goals and desires and where you have talent. Measurement and testing will be periodic and continuous, and the program specifics will be altered over time based on life changes, trending of the measured health and wellness parameters, diet, and the predictability of certain types of diseases and illnesses based on your genome. Synthetic drugs and substances that occur in nature will be viewed and considered equally based on information provided from genetic testing along with the present health and wellness status of the individual. Choices will be quantified along with their risks, potential benefits, and potential consequences. For example, an individual will clearly understand the impact, either positive or negative, of drinking a soda, eating certain foods, smoking a cigarette, or ingesting a synthetic drug.

## *Intersection of Health and the Internet of Things*

Employers and insurance companies could offer a range of health and wellness programs as services. This means the creation of programs that could include a bundled set of offerings with flexible pricing models. The program could include genetic testing, health and wellness checkups, diet and exercise recommendations, and prescription drugs when required. Pricing could include incentives based on your adherence to the program and your ability to maintain measurable wellness performance indicators. Today, technology allows auto insurance companies and automobile manufacturers to track the performance of drivers and the performance and health of the car through a range of parameters and metrics. In addition to traditional methods that the insurance companies are made aware of, such as accidents and traffic tickets, technology is now embedded in the vehicle, allowing the insurance company to monitor your driving habits. The insurance company can tell if you are speeding, how many miles you drive every day, where you drive, and so on. It uses this information to set pricing and create incentives for safe driving. Analytics technology allows the insurance company to gather the data of many drivers and determine a profile or best practice for a "safe driver," along with targets for the key parameters that impact the profile. If you meet or exceed those measurable performance metrics, you may be given a price discount.

The manufacturer of the automobile also has remote access to much of the same data and information from the automobile, which it uses to assess how its cars are performing. This data can also be used by the auto manufacturer to provide insight to its product development teams on how the cars are being used, what changes may be required, and what features may need to be added or modified. The same technology can be used to alert its service teams to specific problems within the car that might require service, the timing for general maintenance, or the prediction of a possible upcoming failure. In this environment, the automobile is continuously communicating with multiple interested parties including the car owner, the insurance company, the automobile manufacturer, and the automobile service provider. In the case of the auto manufacturer, communication may be with multiple constituencies within the company, in this case the product development teams, marketing, sales, and customer support. When technology enables this network effect paradigm to be extended to allow machines to communicate with other machines, you have the basis for the autonomous car, which was mentioned earlier, along with an entire new industry, referred to as the Internet of Things (IoT). Autonomous or self-driving cars leverage a range of video and sensor technologies, along with analytics software, to visualize, sense, and communicate with other sensors, cars, and people.

Aspects of this model are in the early stages of being leveraged to transform healthcare programs and insurance. Just as the vital signs of a car can be logged and tracked, the vital signs and key health indicators of a human can be recorded and tracked. Very popular wearable devices are already enabling this today. Innovative health insurance companies, leveraging powerful software analytics technology along with these devices, can make more accurate risk predictions and reward users of the technology who follow a recommended fitness program. In the future, deviations from a "normal" reading, with normal being partially determined by your genetic testing, would trigger an alert or recommendation on your personal device and perhaps a consultation with a doctor or wellness advisor. Sophisticated analytics software could analyze any deviation in your data in the context of genetics, diet, exercise, and so on to determine potential causes and suggest possible solutions. Just like the automobile example, there may be multiple constituencies interested in your health data, including various doctors and other health professionals, health and wellness coaches, insurance companies, and employers. The most interested party will, of course, be yourself, and you will control how your program is set up and whom your data and information is shared with. Healthcare programs would also include any ongoing genetic testing, doctor visits that could occur locally or remotely from your own home or office, a recommended diet and exercise program tailored to your specific genetic makeup and preferences, and prescribed recommendations that might include natural dietary substances and products, vitamins and other supplements, or synthetic drugs, and wellness treatments such as chiropractic, massage, or acupuncture. With today's technology, not only can vital signs and other health parameters be easily captured and tracked, but it will soon be possible to evaluate and track everything you purchase and consume. Leveraging augmented reality and analytics technologies, you may be able to evaluate the impact of a particular food product in the context of your own personalized wellness program while you are shopping, before you decide to purchase it. Analytics software will be able to gauge the impact of what you consume on your overall health and make recommendations based on what is optimal for you. This same ability to track consumables also applies to exercise options, where you live and travel, and all sorts of other variables that could potentially impact your health and wellness (air and water quality, sun exposure, etc.).

The common denominator, or focus, of this model is you and your overall well-being. In this model, synthetic drugs and their manufacturers, along with big government, are no longer the center of the universe; you and your health are. Drugs are viewed for what they are—a combination of chemicals that have a unique effect on everyone, either positive or negative, just like substances that occur in nature. Computer and analytics technology is leveraged to ensure that anything and everything is evaluated based on the impact on the unique genetic makeup of each individual.

### The Dark Side

This future vision also carries with it several ethical and privacy concerns. Having your health and genetic data tracked, analyzed, and managed will create concerns about who has access and how it is shared and used. The patient will need to be the primary decision-maker in deciding which information is made available to whom. This would also include what is conveyed back to the patient in the case of predictive genetic tests. Some patients may prefer not to be made aware of something in their genome that indicates a negative condition. How will the industry use personal information to price healthcare in a manner that is not only fair and equitable, but also competitive and efficient? Other ethical concerns will arise based on the availability of detailed genetic information. Genetic information could increase the risk of people being discriminated against, especially if that information quantifies specific genetic physical and learning characteristics. How do you ethically deal with genetic information related to young children and the unborn? These questions and issues, along with many others, will need to be addressed as we move forward.

### *Gene Editing and DNA Repair*

Many diseases are the result of genetic disorders or mutations. Examples of genetic disorders include Alzheimer's disease, Crohn's disease, and muscular dystrophy. Understanding the genetic markers to these disorders and the impact of various chemicals and other external factors that may trigger or suppress them will contribute to a more optimal state of well-being. Ultimately, however, repairing the actual genetic damage may be the only way to eliminate the problem. Recently, technology has been introduced allowing targeted genes to be "edited" or DNA to be "repaired"[91]. This technology is nascent but offers hope for people with a family history of genetic disorders. It has also triggered ethical concerns regarding the implications of editing genes that could be passed on to future generations.

## Genetic Reboot

Can genetic mutations caused by diet, sensitivities, or the environment that trigger disease be reversed? Would it be possible to "reboot" or reset genes to correct a genetic mutation in the same way you might reboot your computer to fix a problem? Just like a computer, where a reboot can fix a problem by restarting a malfunctioning piece of hardware, could you fix a genetic mutation by rebooting a gene sequence? Are there natural substances that could potentially facilitate such a process? The questions and the general idea may not be as absurd as it initially sounds, as there are several examples of naturally occurring substances that have been suggested as having such properties. Ayahuasca, although quite controversial, is an example of a plant that some claim has medicinal value[92]. Ayahuasca is found in the Amazon jungles and consists of the ayahuasca vine and a shrub called chacruna, which contains N, N-dimethyltryptamine (DMT), a naturally occurring psychedelic drug of the tryptamine family. DMT is also found in the pineal gland of humans. The pineal gland, a tiny pinecone-shaped gland located in the brain, has been described by some as a link between the physical and spiritual world or a "third eye." This has triggered conspiracy theories, including one suggesting fluoridated water, or medicine water, was used by govern-ments to control the minds of the population by obstructing the function of the pineal gland[93]. Because it contains the psychedelic DMT, ayahuasca is illegal in the United States. Ayahuasca use may have a positive impact on the brain and disorders impacted by the brain structure, or limbic sys-tem, such as anxiety, PTSD, depression, insomnia, various addictions, and other emotional conditions[94]. Is it possible that ayahuasca acts as a reboot to damaged genes and neu-rotransmitters in the brain? In the context of a genetic-cen-tric system, substances such as ayahuasca would be tested to determine potential impact. Testing would include deter-mining how a substance, regardless of whether it is synthetic or occurs in nature, would be accepted by unique individu-als with their own unique genetic makeup and sensitivities.

### *What We Don't Know*

There are close to four hundred thousand different spe-cies of plants on our planet. In 2015, over two thousand new species were discovered[95]. How many of these plants could potentially impact diseases such as cancer? There are numerous claims of plants having some sort of health, well-ness, or medicinal properties. One example is the soursop fruit of the graviola tree, which is found in Latin America, South America, and the Caribbean. Some claim that sour-sop not only has a wide range of health benefits but can also kill cancer cells[96]. Perhaps if big government and pri-vate investment resources were not totally consumed on synthetic drugs and propping up an unsustainable synthetic-drug-based system, we might be able to shift the focus, reallocate investment and capital, and seriously evaluate alternatives. Perhaps a recognition of the potential wellness and medicinal properties of plants would trigger a shift in investment and new economic opportunities to areas such as the Amazon, which contain many species of plants that have yet to even be discovered. These regions would become highly valued as sources for innovative new treatments and cures, instead of bulldozed for agriculture and other purposes.

## *Regenerate*

There are many promising, innovative healthcare and wellness ideas presently being explored and developed, and I can't cover them all in this book. As a final example, regenerative medicine offers the promise of using stem cells to repair the immune system, speed healing, grow new cells, and treat a range of diseases. Stem cells are cells from which all other cells with specialized functions are generated[97]. When our son was born, my wife and I had the umbilical cord blood, which is loaded with vibrant stem cells, harvested and preserved. At some point in his life, my son, or perhaps someone else, may be able to benefit from these stem cells by using them to reverse a chronic disease or treat some other health-related issue. The ability to regenerate new cells, new tissue, even new organs, is no longer something to be found only in science fiction.

## *How Do We Get There?*

Introducing a new order is never easy, especially when the present synthetic-chemical-centric system has powerful interests that will vigorously resist change. Having said that, if our goal is to continuously improve the health and wellness of our families, we must make fundamental changes to transform the present system. The following are suggestions that could help facilitate a discussion and accelerate a transition that is already underway. These ideas aren't original, but they leverage common sense and what has been introduced in this book. They will also have to be formulated not individually, but in the context of a broader integrated system with a focus on your individual genetic profile and optimizing wellness over a lifetime.

### *Start with Wellness*

Policies that encourage and reward wellness should be promoted and incentivized by government, business, the medical establishment, and the insurance industry. Individual, personalized wellness based on your unique genetic makeup is central to transforming our healthcare system. This process is already underway as shown through initiatives that are being driven and tested by innovative individuals and businesses. The opportunity, however, is to accelerate and leverage this trend to drive change in other areas that may be more challenging, such as reducing consumption of synthetic chemicals. As people become more engaged and focused on wellness, they will become more aware of healthier alternatives to the choices provided by the synthetic-chemical-centered establishment. We have discussed some examples of how incentives are applied in the automobile insurance industry and how that could apply to wellness. What must also be factored is the incredible rate of progress and change that is occurring with advancements in technology. Not only is the technology evolving rapidly, but so are the innovative business models and applications of the technology. This is very promising and a harbinger of change for our healthcare system.

## *Genetic Testing for Everyone*

Your own personal genome should be integral to any longer-term wellness program and commitment to a healthier lifestyle. Soon, the sequencing of your genome will serve as a map and a guide to your own personal health and wellness program. While this industry is in its early stages and there are still several issues and questions related to application, accuracy, and ethics, the technology is evolving rapidly and promises to fundamentally change healthcare. The Human Genome Project planted the seeds for this revolution; now policies must encourage and accelerate the leveraging of this technology rather than resist it for the sake of propping up a broken system.

Creating a transformative model could start by establishing an initial health and wellness baseline at a certain age for everyone based on a personal genetic map, vital signs, and other health indicators. A program could be generated to include a recommended diet and exercise regimen based on the initial baseline and the personal goals and preferences of each individual. Performance would be measured and tracked with variants resulting in either positive or negative incentives, financial or otherwise. Your ability to manage your own wellness could impact the price of any service. In the future, insurance companies or other business entities that emerge to provide programs and services should not be allowed to deny service to those with preexisting genetic dispositions. For example, if colon cancer runs in your family and your genetic tests show that you are predisposed to potentially have colon cancer at some stage in your life, you will not be denied the benefits of program coverage as a result. Sophisticated analytics will be able to score everyone based on their genetic makeup, vital signs, and other health factors in the context of the overall population. Government subsidies, if required, for the various programs could be based not only on the financial condition of the individual, but also on the genetic predisposition and baseline wellness of the individual as determined by his or her score.

## *Reengineer the US Patent System for Pharmaceuticals*

The US patent system is the engine that powers the synthetic-drug-centric model that exists today. If we are serious about altering the model, we need to change the primary incentive that drives behavior. Simplification should be the strategy. The first step is to reduce the complexities and variables around the patent awards and the additional exclusivity that is doled out by the FDA. The system as it exists today is a lightning rod for litigation—great for lawyers and extending the duration of drug product monopolies, but bad for consumers and those who foot the bill for it. The second step would be to establish a straightforward period of exclusivity based on when a synthetic drug hits the market—period. No other patents, extensions, variants, or anything else that could extend a monopoly. This period would have to be considerably less than the twenty-year patent issue. We can leave the calculation and debate around the exact amount of time for another day, but it would have to factor in the costs and risks associated with synthetic-drug development against the drag on innovation, competition, and cost to society. One option could be reducing the patent period in exchange for a percentage of sales or profits generated from generic spin-offs of the drug. The key is to establish incentives that will drive innovation, competition, and a more level playing field for alternative, natural products and solutions. Once the incentives are refactored and the complexity that allows the system to be gamed is reduced, investment capital will naturally flow in the direction of better opportunities, opportunities that may not include the proliferation of synthetic drugs.

## _Promotion and Education on Natural Health Solutions_

Substances and treatments that occur in nature can no longer be relegated to second-class status. Whether it is evaluating acupuncture or chiropractic as an alternative to pain relief medication or surgery, or considering red yeast rice, red wine, or garlic instead of statins for high cholesterol, alternative treatments need to be front and center. At a minimum, doctors should be required to inform patients of potential alternatives before they prescribe a drug. And the excuse that natural alternatives aren't "proved" to provide benefits is getting tired, especially when you consider the side effects and negative impacts of so many government-approved chemicals and drugs, issues that often don't manifest themselves until sometime in the distant future. Just as doctors need to make patients aware of natural alternatives, insurance companies need to at least offer coverage options for natural alternatives. From a business perspective, why would an insurance company cover a doctor visit and a drug prescription over an acupuncture treatment that perhaps is more effective and less costly? Could it be that the insurance industry has bought into the same system and dogma that the rest of society has bought into regarding synthetic drugs? The healthier the patient, the lower the cost to the insurance company and the more money the insurance company should make. It has also been proved that businesses save a lot of money by having healthy employees. Not only should businesses pressure government and insurance companies to cover wellness programs and natural treatments, but if the insurance companies won't support them, businesses should consider the investment themselves. Finally, synthetic drugs should not be advertised on television and other forms of media unless equal billing is provided to natural alternatives. Again, I will leave the debate over how this is executed for another day.

## _Program Purchases for Low-Income Citizens_

Why can't big government ever show its love for low-income citizens without creating massive bureaucracies, regulations, and financial burdens on the industries and the companies attempting to provide the goods and services? If you are so concerned about low-income citizens not having health insurance, just buy them a policy. Create laws and regulations that increase competition, not eliminate it so that big government can step in and pronounce an entire industry a failure, with the result being a big-government takeover of the industry and government, of course, running everything. Don't micromanage an entire industry into oblivion by dictating what its products must include and how they are brought to market under the guise of being the noble protector of the poor. If you believe that something is a right, you should first define what "it" is. Is it a right to health insurance? Is it a right to healthcare? Is it a right to a healthier life or lifestyle? If people have a right to a healthier life, pumping them with synthetic chemicals will not achieve the objective. Having big government micromanage, or take over, a component of a broken system also won't solve a problem or achieve an objective; it will just add cost. The result will be a broken system that is less efficient, which would accurately summarize the Affordable Care Act. When big government is unwilling to recognize the underlying cause of a broken system, efforts to reform or improve it are doomed from the beginning. But more activist government involvement in healthcare was never about reform or improvement; it was about government control and power. Assuming you have no intent to reengineer an unsustainable system, or you don't possess the competence to do so, the next best thing would be to define what you are trying to achieve, and when you determine that groups of people can't afford it, simply figure out what it is going to cost to buy it for them. At that point, the only thing left is the actual process for executing the transaction. The hard part for big government is always the "how are you going to pay for it" part. Making hard choices and living within one's means never seem to be serious considerations. Getting the grandchildren to pay for it, in the form of added debt, is the usual outcome. Healthy citizens are going to be more productive citizens, so investing in those citizens is always a good idea, assuming the investment does not include big government as an anchor dragging down citizens, multiple industries, and the economy.

### Our Future

The future does not have to be a continuation of the past. Breakthroughs in genetic engineering, computer science, and software, along with a new awareness of natural alternatives driven by the Internet and increased transparency, provide hope for the future. Our present system is synthetic-chemical-centric, meaning that it is set up and optimized to ensure the maximum use of synthetic-chemical substances and ensure the success and wealth of the companies that manufacture them. The system is managed, sustained, and protected by big government, which derives money and power from the partnership. Changing the system first requires a clear understanding of the system and what drives it. It also requires a vision for a better system to replace it and a plan to make the transition. We should not expect or wait for a new system and a plan to enable it to come from loving big government. Innovation will be driven by private individuals, businesses, nonprofits, researchers, and anyone who has a passion for improving health and wellness. The ideas and technology that originate and are nurtured from these groups will ultimately drive the transition to a new system and model for health and wellness. Hopefully, this book provides a better understanding of the existing system along with a starting point for developing and implementing something better that will lead to a healthier, longer life for our families and future generations.

# NOTES

1.  "What Are the Possible Causes of ADHD?" Shire US, accessed April 10, 2017, https://www.adhdadulthood.com/en/adult-adhd/what-causes-adhd

2.  "Healthcare Industry Statistics," Statistic Brain Research Institute, September 25, 2016, http://www.statisticbrain.com/health-care-industry-statistics/

3.  "National Health Expenditure Data," Centers for Medicare and Medicaid Services, accessed April 15, 2017, https://www.cms.gov/Research-Statistics-Data-and-Systems/Statistics-Trends-and-Reports/NationalHealthExpendData/

4.  "U.S. Pharmaceutical Industry - Statistics and Facts," The Statistics Portal, accessed April 15, 2017, https://www.statista.com/topics/1719/pharmaceutical-industry/

5.  "Total Global Spending on Pharmaceutical Research and Development," The Statistics Portal, accessed April 15, 2017, https://www.statista.com/statistics/309466/global-r-and-d-expenditure-for-pharmaceuticals/

6. "2016 Top Markets Report Pharmaceuticals," International Trade Administration, Department of Commerce, accessed April 15, 2017, http://www.trade.gov/topmarkets/pdf/Pharmaceuticals_Executive_Summary.pdf

7. "Policy Basics: Where do Federal Tax Revenues Come From?" Center on Budget and Policy Priorities, last modified March 4, 2016, http://www.cbpp.org/research/policy-basics-where-do-federal-tax-revenues-come-from

8. "Tax Rates by Sector," Stern NYU, last modified January 2017, http://pages.stern.nyu.edu/~adamodar/New_Home_Page/datafile/taxrate.htm

9. "Lobbying: Top Industries," Center for Responsive Politics, accessed April 15, 2017, https://www.opensecrets.org/lobby/top.php?showYear=2016&indexType=i

10. "Persuading the Prescribers: Pharmaceutical Marketing and its Influence on Physicians and Patients," The Pew Charitable Trusts, last modified November 11, 2013, http://www.pewtrusts.org/en/research-and-analysis/fact-sheets/2013/11/11/persuading-the-prescribers-pharmaceutical-industry-marketing-and-its-influence-on-physicians-and-patients

11. "Pharmaceutical Industry Gets High on Fat Profits," BBC News, GlobalData, November 6, 2014, http://www.bbc.com/news/business-28212223

12. "Margins by Sector", Stern NYU, last modified January 2017, http://pages.stern.nyu.edu/~adamodar/New_Home_Page/datafile/margin.html

13. "Frequently Asked Questions on Patents and Exclusivity," U.S. Food and Drug Administration, last modified December 5, 2016, https://www.fda.gov/Drugs/DevelopmentApprovalProcess/ucm079031.htm

14. "Types of Pharmaceutical Patents," O'Brien Patent Solutions, accessed April 17, 2017, http://www.obrienpatents.com/types-pharmaceutical-patents/

15. "New Drug Approval Process," Drugs.com, accessed April 17, 2017, https://www.drugs.com/fda-approval-process.html

16. "Who Funds Biomedical Research?" The Balance, Kathlyn Stone, last modified April 24, 2017, https://www.thebalance.com/who-funds-biomedical-research-2663193

17. "This Is Why Your Drug Prescriptions Cost So Damn Much," Mother Jones, Stuart Silverstein, Fairwarning, October 21, 2016, http://www.motherjones.com/politics/2016/10/drug-industry-pharmaceutical-lobbyists-medicare-part-d-prices/

18. "H.R.1 – Medicare Prescription Drug, Improvement, and Modernization Act of 2003," Congress.gov, accessed April 19, 2017, https://www.congress.gov/bill/108th-congress/house-bill/1

19. "Patent Expiration and Pharmaceutical Prices," The National Bureau of Economic Research, Linda Gorman, accessed April 22, 2017, http://www.nber.org/digest/sep14/w20016.html

20. "United States Life Tables 2012," Centers for Disease Control, National Vital Statistics Reports, November 28, 2016, https://www.cdc.gov/nchs/data/nvsr/nvsr65/nvsr65_08.pdf

21. "Carbohydrates and Blood Sugar," Harvard T.H. Chan, The Nutrition Source, accessed April 29, 2017, https://www.hsph.harvard.edu/nutritionsource/carbohydrates/carbohydrates-and-blood-sugar/

22. "10 Reasons Why Sugar is Bad For You," Authority Nutrition, Kris Gunnars, BSc, September 30, 2013, https://authoritynutrition.com/10-disturbing-reasons-why-sugar-is-bad/

23. "Does Inflammation Trigger Insulin Resistance and Diabetes?" Scientific America, Melinda Wenner, December 1, 2009, https://www.scientificamerican.com/article/inflammatory-clues/

24. "Food Guide Pyramid," United States Department of Agriculture, accessed April 30, 2017, https://www.cnpp.usda.gov/FGP

25. "Calcium and Strong Bones," Physicians Committee for Responsible Medicine, accessed April 30, 2017, http://www.pcrm.org/health/health-topics/calcium-and-strong-bones

26. "The History of Raw Milk and Pasteurization," Food (Policy) for Thought, May 6, 2014, http://foodpolicyforthought.com/2014/05/06/the-history-of-raw-milk-and-pasteurization/

27. "US Sales of Dairy Milk Turn Sour As Non-Dairy Milk Sales Grow 9% in 2015," Mintel, April 20, 2016, http://www.mintel.com/press-centre/food-and-drink/us-sales-of-dairy-milk-turn-sour-as-non-dairy-milk-sales-grow-9-in-2015

28. "Where is it all coming From," healthline, accessed April 30, 2017, http://www.healthline.com/health/high-fructose-corn-syrup-or-sugar#where-does-it-come-from4

29. "What is Cholesterol," National Institutes of Health, accessed April 30, 2017, https://www.nhlbi.nih.gov/health/health-topics/topics/hbc/

30. "Is Butter Really Back?" Harvard T.H. Chan, accessed June 20, 2017, https://www.hsph.harvard.edu/magazine/magazine_article/is-butter-really-back/

31. "New evidence raises questions about the link between fatty acids and heart disease," University of Cambridge, accessed June 20, 2017, http://www.cam.ac.uk/research/news/new-evidence-raises-questions-about-the-link-between-fatty-acids-and-heart-disease

32. "Interesterification – The Dangerous Replacement for Trans Fats," Natural News, Frank Cooper, March 3, 2008, http://www.naturalnews.com/022759_oil_fat_oils.html

33. "Frequently Asked Questions," Fluoride Action Network, accessed May 2, 2017, http://fluoridealert.org/faq/

34. "Facts About Fluoridation," LiveScience, Douglas Main, April 30, 2015, https://www.livescience.com/37123-fluoridation.html

35. "Fluoridation Chemicals," Second Look, accessed May 2, 2017, http://www.slweb.org/chemicals.html

36. "National Research Council (2006)," Fluoride Action Network, accessed May 2, 2017, http://fluoridealert.org/researchers/nrc/findings/

37. "Follow The Money: Who Profits From Fluoridation? And Who Pays?" Secure Arkansas, accessed May 2, 2017, https://securetherepublic.com/arkansas/2015/07/08/follow-the-money-who-profits-from-fluoridation-and-who-pays/

38. "Top 10 Reasons To Go Organic," Prevention, Renee Loux, November 3, 2011, http://www.prevention.com/food/healthy-eating-tips/top-reasons-choose-organic-foods

39. "Growth Opportunities in the Global Pesticide Industry 2016 – 2021," Cision PR Newswire, Lucintel, September 5, 2016, http://www.prnewswire.com/news-releases/growth-opportunities-in-the-global-pesticide-industry-2016-2021-trends-forecast-and-opportunity-analysis-august-2016-300322619.html

40. "Bisphenol A and Hormone-Associated Cancers: Current Progress and Perspectives," NCBI, January 9, 2015, https://www.ncbi.nlm.nih.gov/pmc/articles/PMC4602822/

41. "Indoor Air Pollution Worse Than Outdoor," Dr. Axe, accessed May 3, 2017, https://draxe.com/indoor-air-pollution-worse-than-outdoor/

42. "Why do Americans spend so much on pharmaceuticals?" PBS Newshour, Valerie Paris, February 7, 2014, http://www.pbs.org/newshour/updates/americans-spend-much-pharmaceuticals/

43. "Therapeutic Drug Use," Centers for Disease Control and Prevention, last modified January 19, 2017, https://www.cdc.gov/nchs/fastats/drug-use-therapeutic.htm

44. "How Many Pills Do Your Elderly Patients Take Each Day?" MD Magazine, last modified October 4, 2010, http://www.mdmag.com/conference-coverage/aafp_2010/how-many-pills-do-your-elderly-patients-take-each-day

45. "The Elderly Are Taking Too Many Pills," HuffPost, Ann Brenoff, last modified June 30, 2015, http://www.huffingtonpost.com/ann-brenoff/elderly-taking-too-many-pills_b_7079060.html

46. "FAERS by Patient Outcomes by Year," U.S. Food and Drug Administration, last modified November 24, 2015, https://www.fda.gov/drugs/guidancecomplianceregulatoryinformation/surveillance/adversedrugeffects/ucm070461.htm

47. "2015 Brought Biggest Percent Increase In Traffic Deaths In 50 Years," Newsweek, Stan Ziv, February 17, 2016, http://www.newsweek.com/2015-brought-biggest-us-traffic-death-increase-50-years-427759

48. "Food Allergy Deaths: Less Common Than You Think," HuffPost, Meredith Broussard, last modified November 17, 2011, http://www.huffingtonpost.com/meredith-broussard/food-allergy-deaths-less_b_151462.html

49. "Prescription Drug User Fee Act (PDUFA)," U.S. Food and Drug Administration, last modified June 21, 2017, https://www.fda.gov/forindustry/userfees/prescriptiondruguserfee/

50. "How Much Money Do Drug Companies Pay the FDA," PLOS Blogs, Jessica Wapner, January 25, 2012, http://blogs.plos.org/workinprogress/2012/01/25/how-much-money-do-drug-companies-pay-the-fda/

51. "FDA takes action to protect consumers from dangerous dietary supplements," U.S. Food and Drug Administration, last modified December 18, 2015, https://www.fda.gov/newsevents/newsroom/pressannouncements/ucm473099.htm

52. "Do You Have Enough HCL (Stomach Acid)?" Branch Basics, accessed May 7, 2015, https://branchbasics.com/do-you-have-enough-hcl-stomach-acid/

53. "Risks associated with common acid-suppressing medications documented in series of studies," ScienceDaily, JAMA and Archive

Journals, May 11, 2010, https://www.sciencedaily.com/releases/2010/05/100510161248.htm

54. "Probiotic effects on intestinal fermentation patterns in patients with irritable bowel syndrome." U.S. National Library of Medicine, PubMed, August 28, 2008, https://www.ncbi.nlm.nih.gov/pubmed/18763284

55. "What Is Your Gut Telling You?" WebMD, Sonya Collins, August 20, 2014, http://www.webmd.com/digestive-disorders/news/20140820/your-gut-bacteria#1

56. "Predisease: A concept whose time has come?" Clinical Advisor, Ronald L. Hoffman, MD, February 16, 2012, http://www.clinicaladvisor.com/features/predisease-a-concept-whose-time-has-come/article/228117/

57. "Low Dose Aspirin For Heart Attack Protection Is Dangerous- Learn Why," Natural Society, Paul Fassa, December 22, 2011, http://naturalsociety.com/why-daily-low-dose-aspirin-for-heart-attack-protection-should-be-discouraged/

58. "Vital Signs (Body Temperature, Pulse Rate, Respiration Rate, Blood Pressure)," Johns Hopkins Medicine, accessed May 7, 2017, http://www.hopkinsmedicine.org/healthlibrary/conditions/adult/cardiovascular_diseases/vital_signs_body_temperature_pulse_rate_respiration_rate_blood_pressure_85,p00866/

59. "Shaking up the Salt Myth: The Dangers of Salt Restriction," Chris Kresser, April 20, 2012, https://chriskresser.com/shaking-up-the-salt-myth-the-dangers-of-salt-restriction/

60. "Understanding Blood Oxygen Levels at Rest," FitDay, accessed May 10, 2017, http://www.fitday.com/fitness-articles/fitness/cardio/understanding-blood-oxygen-levels-at-rest.html

61. "The drug industry's answer to opioid addiction: More pills," The Washington Post, Ariana Eunjung Cha, October 16, 2016, https://www.washingtonpost.com/national/the-drug-industrys-answer-to-opioid-addiction-more-pills/2016/10/15/181a529c-8ae4-11e6-bff0-d53f592f176e_story.html?utm_term=.8ff2cee4d345

62. "How is heroin linked to prescription drug abuse?" National Institute on Drug Abuse, accessed May 10, 2017, https://www.drugabuse.gov/publications/research-reports/heroin/how-heroin-linked-to-prescription-drug-abuse

63. "Increases in Drug and Opioid Overdose Deaths – United States, 2000-2014," Centers for Disease Control and Prevention, January 1, 2016, https://www.cdc.gov/mmwr/preview/mmwrhtml/mm6450a3.htm

64. "Making the Vaccine Decision," Centers for Disease Control and Prevention, last modified May 11, 2017, https://www.cdc.gov/vaccines/parents/vaccine-decision/index.html

65. "Influenza Deaths: The Hype vs. The Evidence," National Vaccine Information Center, Barbara Loe Fisher, October 3, 2012, http://www.nvic.org/NVIC-Vaccine-News/October-2012/Influenza-Deaths--The-Hype-vs--The-Evidence.aspx#comments

66. "Vaccines for preventing influenza in healthy adults." NCBI PubMed, July 7, 2010, https://www.ncbi.nlm.nih.gov/pubmed/20614424

67. "Estimating Seasonal Influenza-Associated Deaths in the United States," Centers for Disease Control and Prevention, last modified December 9, 2016, https://www.cdc.gov/flu/about/disease/us_flu-related_deaths.htm

68. "IMS Health Study: Global Market for Cancer Treatments Grows to $107 Billion in 2015, Fueled by Record Level of Innovation," QuintilesIMS, June 2, 2016, http://www.imshealth.com/en/about-us/news/ims-health-study-global-market-for-cancer-treatments-grows-to-107-billion-in-2015-fueled-by-record-level-of-innovation

69. "Cancer Stat Facts: Cancer of Any Site," NIH, National Cancer Institute, accessed May 13, 2017, https://seer.cancer.gov/statfacts/html/all.html

70. "What is Cancer?" National Cancer Institute, last modified February 9, 2015, https://www.cancer.gov/about-cancer/understanding/what-is-cancer

71. "Viruses that can lead to cancer," American Cancer Society, last modified July 11, 2016, https://www.cancer.org/cancer/cancer-causes/infectious-agents/infections-that-can-lead-to-cancer/viruses.html

72. "Virus", The Free Dictionary, accessed May 14, 2015, http://medical-dictionary.thefreedictionary.com/virus

73. "What causes cancer?" Cancer Tutor, last modified June 14, 2017, https://www.cancertutor.com/what_causes_cancer/

74. "A to Z List of Cancer Drugs," NIH National Cancer Institute, last modified May 19, 2017, https://www.cancer.gov/about-cancer/treatment/drugs

75. "High Dose Vitamin C," NIH National Cancer Institute, last modified April 20, 2017, https://www.cancer.gov/about-cancer/treatment/cam/patient/vitamin-c-pdq

76. "Is Vitamin C Cancer Therapy Effective?" The Truth About Cancer, accessed May 13, 2017, https://thetruthaboutcancer.com/vitamin-c-cancer-therapy/

77. "Creative Destruction," Library of Economics and Liberty, W. Michael Cox and Richard Alm, accessed May 16, 2017, http://www.econlib.org/library/Enc/CreativeDestruction.html

78. "Affordable Care Act (ACA)," Healthcare.gov, accessed May 16, 2017, https://www.healthcare.gov/glossary/affordable-care-act/

79. "Medicare and Medicaid: What's the Difference?" NOLO, accessed May 16, 2017, http://www.nolo.com/legal-encyclopedia/medicare-medicaid-whats-difference-29615.html

80. "Obamacare's Medicaid expansion leading to health insurance boom in some states," CNBC, Dan Mangan, July 20, 2016, http://www.cnbc.com/2016/07/20/obamacares-medicaid-expansion-leading-to-health-insurance-boom-in-some-states.html

81. "Cost of Obamacare Medicaid Expansion 49% Higher Than Previously Estimated," cnsnews.com, Ricardo Alonso-Zaldivar, August 12, 2016,

http://www.cnsnews.com/news/article/medicaid-estimate-renews-cost-concerns-over-obamacare

82. "Health Policy Brief," Health Affairs, Julia James, February 25, 2016, http://healthaffairs.org/healthpolicybriefs/brief_pdfs/healthpolicy-brief_153.pdf

83. "The Rising Cost of Healthcare by Year and Its Causes," the balance, Kimberly Amadeo, last modified June 21, 2017, https://www.thebalance.com/causes-of-rising-healthcare-costs-4064878

84. "How Many Are Newly Insured As A Result Of The ACA?" American Action Forum, Tara O'Neill Hayes, January 4, 2017, https://www.americanactionforum.org/insight/20-million/

85. "genomics," TechTarget Network, last modified December, 2015, http://searchhealthit.techtarget.com/definition/genomics

86. "genome," Vocabulary.com, accessed May 20, 2017, https://www.vocabulary.com/dictionary/genome

87. "The Human Genome Project Completion: Frequently Asked Questions," National Human Genome Research Institute, last modified October 30, 2010, https://www.genome.gov/11006943/human-genome-project-completion-frequently-asked-questions/

88. "What is a genome?" yg, last modified January 6, 2017, http://www.yourgenome.org/facts/what-is-a-genome

89. "Your smartphone is millions of times more powerful than all of NASA's combined computing in 1969," ZME Science, last modified May 17, 2017, http://www.zmescience.com/research/technology/smartphone-power-compared-to-apollo-432/

90. "Moore's Law," Moore's Law, accessed May 26, 2017, http://www.mooreslaw.org/

91. "What is CRISPR-Cas9?" yg, last modified December 19, 2016, http://www.yourgenome.org/facts/what-is-crispr-cas9

92. "The Ayahuasca Experience," Reality Sandwich, Chris Kilham, accessed May 28, 2017, http://realitysandwich.com/235051/the-ayahuasca-experience/

93. "Pineal Gland Our Third Eye: The Biggest cover up in human history," Mystic Banana, accessed May 28, 2017, http://www.mysticbanana.com/pineal-gland-our-third-eye-the-biggest-cover-up-in-human-history.html

94. "Study: Long-Term Use of Ayahuasca Linked To Changes In Personality And Brain Structure," reset.me, Dale Richardson, Ph.D., October 23, 2015, http://reset.me/study/study-long-term-use-of-ayahuasca-linked-to-changes-in-personality-and-brain-structure/

95. "How many different plants are there in the world?" siliconrepublic, Gordon Hunt, May 10, 2016, https://www.siliconrepublic.com/discovery/how-many-plants-are-there-in-the-world

96. "27 Amazing Benefits Of Soursop For Skin, Hair, and Health," stylecraze, Saba, June 20, 2017, http://www.stylecraze.com/articles/benefits-of-soursop-for-skin-hair-and-health/

97. "Stem cells: What they are and what they do," Mayo Clinic, March 23, 2013, http://www.mayoclinic.org/tests-procedures/bone-marrow-transplant/in-depth/stem-cells/art-20048117